on purpose

living life as it was intended

Jonny Ivey

To Josiah,

This book is two days older than you. We pray
that you too would come to enjoy life as it was
intended, like all else, to the glory of God.
– Jonny Ivey

CruciformPress

"It is an inescapable aspect of the human condition to reflect on the meaning and purpose of our lives. Many strive to achieve status or attain happiness, whilst others conclude that life is ultimately meaningless. Combining faithful biblical exegesis with engaging creativity and personal honesty, Jonny Ivey helps us to understand that we were created to glorify God and enjoy him forever. This is a liberating book that will help Christians to find true joy whilst they are being restored into the image of God and wait for the glorious new creation to come."

John Stevens, National Director, Fellowship of Independent Evangelical Churches (UK)

"To understand one's purpose, one must understand the One who designed and created us in his image. Too often, we disconnect our purpose as human beings from who God is. To help bridge that gap, Jonny Ivey has written a book that helps readers navigate some of the most important questions we ask. Ivey packs a punch in this short but brief book. Don't let it's brevity belie the immensity of the subject at hand; take up and read, and be refreshed and reminded of the beauty of being made in the image of God."

Jonathan D. Holmes, Pastor of Counseling, Parkside Church; Executive Director, Fieldstone Counseling

Table of Contents

Cruciform Press

We like to keep it simple. So we publish short, clear, useful, inexpensive books for Christians and other curious people. Books that make sense and are easy to read, even as they tackle serious subjects.

We do this because the good news of Jesus Christ—the gospel—is the only thing that actually explains why this world is so wonderful and so awful all at the same time. Even better, the gospel applies to every single area of life, and offers real answers that aren't available from any other source.

These are books you can afford, enjoy, finish easily, benefit from, and remember. Check us out and see.

On Purpose: Living Life as It Was Intended

Print / PDF ISBN: 978-1-941114-67-4
Mobipocket ISBN: 978-1-941114-68-1
ePub ISBN: 978-1-941114-69-8

ONE

For All Intents and Purposes

Hi. We've not met. I know almost nothing about you. I don't know your name or your age or even your gender. I don't know how you like your tea or if you even like tea. (I hear that some people don't?) I certainly don't know what you believe about the bigger questions of life. But there is something I know about you.

You believe in purpose.

I mean, you're reading a book, right? You picked it up for some purpose or another. Not just because it's about purpose—the same would be true if you'd watched a movie. Or put some bread in the toaster. Or brushed your teeth. Nobody brushes their teeth for no purpose. That would be weird. Why not finish up by brushing your knees? No. We don't do stuff at random. We do it *on purpose*.

This morning I got out of bed, not aimlessly, but because I had things to do. I ate some breakfast, not arbitrarily, but so that I'd have energy for the day. I chose this coffee shop because I like the coffee here, better than the one next door. I ordered a flat white because it tastes better than the cappuccino. I'm now writing this sentence, like everything else today, for a particular reason—to show that whatever we do, we do it purposefully.

Purpose in a Box

Or so I thought. One day I was just happily wandering back to London Waterloo train station when I saw him. A man sitting in a glass box suspended thirty feet above the River Thames. Seemingly unaware of the screaming crowd below, he was staring across the river toward the iconic Tower Bridge. An American tourist, I assumed. In a box?

"It's David Blaine, the American magician guy," said a voice from my left. The balding man must have noticed the confusion on my face. "He's spending six weeks in there with no food, just water," he said, opening a bacon, lettuce, and tomato sandwich.

Now, you can call me conservative but it's not glaringly obvious to me why someone would sit in a box, thirty feet in the air, with no food, for six weeks. Or six days. Or even six minutes. If there was ever an act of supreme pointlessness this was surely it, right?

Wrong.

Blaine wasn't a prisoner. Before he began his stunt, a London journalist asked him why he would put himself through it and he responded calmly and candidly:

> "I think when you have nothing, when you're living with nothing, there's no distractions, you're just there as you are, almost struggling. I think that's the purest state that we can be in." [1]

Looks can be deceiving. It turns out that Blaine wasn't doing his self-starvation, jack-in-a-box stunt for nothing. Quite apart from the fact he has built an international career on these exercises in the unusual, I believe him when he suggests that his reason for doing this ran a little deeper than my choosing a flat white or your decision to pick up a book. Blaine climbed into his glass box to escape everything that wasn't his mind, body, or soul in order to experience his "purest" humanity. That is, the ultimate purpose of being human. No frills. No extras. No iOS updates. Which all sounds very profound but it's actually what you and I are doing every day. We all climb into our glass boxes. We just call them something different.

What Are You Living For?

To experience his purest human purpose, Blaine
climbed into an empty box; we normally fill ours to
the brim. Experiences. Approval. Pleasure. Success.
Stuff. Comfort. Technology. Relationships. Recogni-
tion. Reward. What is true of picking up a book is true
of our lives as a whole. We're living for something. We
are trying to achieve something. We're desperate that
our lives are not pointless, that they count for something. *We want purpose.* Well, what about you? What
are you living for?

I remember that question well. During my first
month at university, the student pastor offered to take
me out for coffee. Because flat whites didn't exist yet in
the UK, I sat down and began to draw patterns in the
frothed milk of my cappuccino. Then he just came out
with it.

"What are you living for, Jonny?"

Now, for anyone who doesn't originate from this
neck of the global woods, let me just fill you in. We
Brits like to talk about the weather. We discuss tea
and cricket (Wikipedia it—or just imagine the Queen
playing baseball). We're not so great at saying we're
happy or sad, much less discussing the existential
foundations underpinning our broken lives. But he
asked it. And the same silent glare of youthful naiveté
would have come his way in response had he asked in

Arabic. I had no idea. Something about Jesus, maybe?

His question didn't go away. It did the rounds in my mind for some months. What *was* I living for? I knew I had come to university in order to get a degree. In order to get a job. In order to have a family. In order to, in order to, in order to, but then what? In order to ultimately do what? To be what? To have what?

I wanted to be married. I wanted children. If possible, they'd be better behaved than other children, on their way to Oxford or Cambridge. I wanted a respected job where I would demonstrate enough leadership to be thought of as successful, and enough subordination to be deemed humble. I wanted a house, big enough to speak of God's undeserved kindness, but small enough to be seen as living radically. I wanted a church, blessed enough by good teaching to call it home, but needy enough that I'd be considered necessary. I wanted to have friends I could speak to about trivial struggles so that in comparison I would look godly, honest, and accountable. This was the glass box that I had entered in order to achieve a purposeful life—not in front of crowds of people, but in the depths of my own hungry heart. In short, I wanted to be someone to others. I wanted people to celebrate me. That's what I was living for. "*Who* are you living for, Jonny?" may have been a better question.

Even twelve years on it feels brutally arrogant writing that down on paper. It would feel even more brutal to say that I still seek purpose in many of the same ways. I still want people to like me and think that I'm a godly, successful, humble kind of a guy. I even want you to like me—and I haven't even met you. I still want to be recognized. To achieve stuff so that people will notice when I enter a room. How could I feel like my life is purposeful if nobody knows me? If the world is unchanged by my existence? If I have nothing to show for my days? Sound familiar at all? Maybe. But if nothing had changed in twelve years I would tell you to close the book now. It wouldn't be worth your time. But fortunately, that's not the end of the story. For me, it was just the beginning.

The Purposeful God

This is a book about purpose. More than that it's a book about what the God of the universe says about purpose. "In the beginning, God created" (Genesis 1:1). It's hardly surprising that as those made in this God's image, we all pursue purpose. The first line of Scripture speaks of a purposeful God. *He created.* Have you ever created something for no purpose whatsoever? Not even because you enjoyed creating it? Have you ever cooked a meal with no regard for how it tastes? Decorated a bedroom, paying no attention to how it looks? Built a Lego house with no care that it should look like one? No. We create meals, homes, computer games, paintings, even Play-Doh models for all intents and purposes—from mere enjoyment, to nourishing our bodies, to making things beautiful. In the same way, God created the world on purpose and stamped his purposeful image all over it.

You only need to read on a few verses to see what he says to us humans, whom he'd just created. We'll see shortly how God told them to subdue the earth and rule over it. God's saying, "Go do something." Go make culture. Make milkshakes. Work and play, eat and drink. Do.

But why? For what purpose? For any we choose? Can we really do whatever we want in his world?

Thankfully God doesn't just give us his world. He gives us his word, in a book. In it he tells us what his world is for. Why he created us. What *we* are for. Have you ever stopped and asked yourself that question? *What am I for?* Is what you're *living* for actually what you're *for*? Are you sure? Well, you *can* be because God's word gives us answers. It doesn't leave us unsure. This is the purpose of God's book: to understand the purpose of books. And everything else in God's world. Including your life and mine.

Can you imagine how David Blaine must have felt coming out of that box after six weeks? The vast expanse must have felt like pure freedom. The first morsel of bread must have been a feast. The first sip of juice like honey. You see, God doesn't invite us to switch from one little box to another. He invites us to step out of our own constricting, claustrophobic box and into our truest, purest human purpose—to enjoy life as it was intended, to come to the feast of his finest produce and the sweetness of eternal joy. It's quite an offer, I'm sure you'll agree.

TWO

What Am I For?

I was one of *them*. You know the type, right? The guy who first stumbles across clear Bible teaching only to stumble over his pride, thinking he's found something nobody else has. That was me; the abrasive, let-me-help-you-out-with-that-speck-in-your-eye, ESV-carrying Christian type. And, I'd just arrived back on campus. Bible in hand.

That night we ferried to church a group of freshmen—"the Fresh," as we called them. We were going through the motions, chatting about what course they'd chosen and where they were from. Before long, an Australian freshman, impatient with the niceties we Brits feel bound by, piped up from the back.

"So fellas," unaware of the three girls walking next to me, "my roommate saw my Bible last night and asked me to show him a verse about the purpose of life." We'd suddenly erred a few steps from social convention. "Anyone got any ideas?"

Readjusting from the sudden turn of conversation, I judged myself the man for the job. It just so happened that I had a few ideas on a vast array of topics I knew nothing about—not least, the purpose of humanity.

"The chief end of man is to glorify God and enjoy him forever," I smiled, glorifying myself and enjoying the precision of my response. I'd read it somewhere. It sounded good. Tuition fees well spent and all that.

"OK," he said with his thick, Sydney accent. "So, what does that mean?"

The truth? I had no idea.

Glory is a spiritual-sounding word that we often use yet know little about. As a kid, I was told once to give God the glory, unaware that I had taken it from him, or where I'd put it. But whenever we speak about human purpose, we can't avoid glory. It sounds erudite, but it's not. It's actually quite mundane. Whether I realized it or not, my wanting to answer the Australian guy's question was all about glory.

The satisfaction of tucking into a Krispy Kreme original glazed donut is all about glory. Glory is about something or someone being good or worthy of praise. We get annoyed or angry when something lacks glory—the car that keeps breaking down, the latest terrorist attack. Glory is about as common to us as the air we breathe. Your eyes see these words because of God's glory. His glory is the reason the sky hasn't fallen in on itself and your lungs still feed on oxygen.

He created the world and us for one purpose—to glorify him.

What does *that* mean?

Well, without giving free rein to my inner grammar geek, when you see the word *glory* in the Old Testament, it has the sense of something—or Someone—being heavy. In the New Testament, the word also carries the sense of reputation. Therefore, we "glorify God" when we make God heavy in our own sight, and in the eyes of others. Jesus commands, "Let your light shine before others, that they may see your good deeds and glorify your Father in heaven" (Matthew 5:16). He's commanding us to bring others to an understanding of God's transforming work in our lives, so that they will give him the full weight of honor and credit he deserves. When we do everything for God's glory, then, whatever we do, we do in such a way that God's weighty splendor shines through and he is given all the credit.[2]

To many people, God is a lightweight. It doesn't really matter what he wants or thinks, or even that he exists. But the purpose of all his creation, especially humanity, is for him to receive glory. And one of the primary ways we as humans glorify him is *to be like him*.

God's Artwork

My Grandad was a professional artist based in South Africa. He did portraits and sketches, oil paintings and pastel scenes. Everything you'd expect of an artist, I guess. He was good—not so good at passing the genes down this direction, but good at his trade nonetheless. My parents hung many of his landscapes on the walls of my childhood home. But one painting stood out. It wasn't a pastel scene or a landscape. It was a large portrait. In prime position overlooking the stairs hung the profile of an elegant woman in her twenties. It was my Gran. His wife. His masterpiece. It was arguably his best work, but that's not why we hung it there. We did so because it was a picture of someone supremely valuable to us. By painting her, my Grandad was saying, "Here's someone worth looking at." By hanging it up, we were enjoying her, honoring her, thanking her, and in a sense glorifying her. Which brings me to the point.

> God said, "Let us make mankind in our image, in our likeness, so that they may rule over the fish in the sea and the birds in the sky, over the livestock and all the wild animals, and over all the creatures that move along the ground." (Genesis 1:26)

God's an artist. He too did landscapes. In the beginning he painted the heavens and the earth. But like my

Grandad, his masterpiece was a portrait. He made us in his own image. We are each a kind of self-portrait of God. Of course, this describes what we are, but it also explains what we are *for*. Our purpose is to be visible pictures of the invisible glory of God. That is, our humanity inevitably looks outward, to God. You exist for the same reason as the picture above our stairs—to enjoy, look to, honor, praise, thank, and resemble someone supremely valuable. To glorify God is to resemble him, to *be* like him. *That* is what you're for.

Maybe the thought of being like this God doesn't excite you. Perhaps all this talk of God creating us and the world for his own glory makes him sound like a lonely egocentric who tapes Polaroid selfies to every wall of his home. But that's not what the God of the Bible is like. He's the unchanging, eternal Reality, of which you and I are a kind of copy. Being made in his image means that whatever you think is good and glorious you'll ultimately find *in* him and by being *like* him. And that's pretty exciting.

But consider this: if *your* inherent nature is to look outward to God, how much more the God you image? In fact, this God is beautifully other-centered. Here's what I mean.

Did you notice how God said, "Let *us* make mankind in *our* image"? That's because, even though he's one God, he's a loving community of three persons—Father, Son, and Spirit. It's impossible to be other-centered without community. God didn't create us because he was lonely or bored. Before he created the world, the persons of this community were enjoying the gloriously sweet and satisfying intimacy of relationship with each other. Nor did he create us because he was selfish in that grubby, grasping way people can be. The Father, Son, and Spirit have eternally been praising, blessing, serving, and glorifying each other (John 17:24). It's this other-centered, outward-looking God who gave us his image. This joy and other-centered nature are of the essence of who he is.

For us, sharing in this joyful union goes well beyond our wildest dreams. It's where all our dreams come from.

So get excited, because here's where it gets good. God, being who he is, wanted to share his joy and the glory of his character. God's glory literally overflowed when he created the world. That's why everything exists for his glory; why we exist for his glory. He stamps his glorious image on us and says, in effect, "Here is your purpose: *to be like me*, because it's so gloriously good" (see Genesis 1:27, 31).

The Bible speaks of many specific ways we can glorify God, but in this book I will be focusing on those two aspects: glorifying God by being like him *in his joy*, and *in his loving character*. I believe they are of primary importance and can serve as a summary of all the Bible says about glorifying God.

Be Like Him in His Joy

How can we be like God in his joy? Well, God has given us this amazing piece of art called the world so we can take joy in it, and thereby be like him. In his joy.

> The heavens declare the glory of God; the skies proclaim the work of his hands. Day after day they pour forth speech; night after night they reveal knowledge. (Psalm 19:1–2)

Both you and I know that we can read about the joy and glory of the Trinity, have a yawn, then go do the dishes. It's impossible for us finite beings to grasp the fullness of the infinite God. So God gives us the gift of his creation so we creatures can understand and participate in his joy. According to Psalm 19, it's an amazing gift that reveals his glory and communicates to us who he is and the joy of being in relationship with him.

This means that the world has real purpose. The purpose of fruit, Oreos, and honey is to reveal to us the sweetness and satisfaction of God. The skies, stars, and seas exist to reveal his power. The green grass, pink sunset, and Neptune's blue were designed to reveal his beauty. Our communities, marriages, and friendships are intended to reveal the glory of his faithful, other-centered character. And in creating all this, he has also given us eyes and ears, hearts and minds, so we can begin to have some grasp of the joy of sharing his image: joyful, satisfied, full. When we open our eyes, ears, mouths, hearts, and hands to the glories of the creation, and especially our fellow image-bearers, we are literally participating in God's glory.

Being like God means that we should enjoy his creation as a way of enjoying *him*. This is what the Father, Son, and Spirit have always been doing. We shouldn't eat a Big Mac and then worship Ronald McDonald. Our satisfaction in the Big Mac reminds us of our satisfaction in God. So we praise him. The beauty of our spouse doesn't mean we should worship him or her. It points us to how beautiful our God is. So we praise him. Our joy in creation is not an end in itself. The joy of country walks, cake, sex, video games, money, literature—they allow us to participate in his joy by praising him. They are glorious gifts that God has given to us so we can give him the glory for it all, and thus enjoy life as he intended. Our purpose is to glorify him by being like him in his joy.

So you're allowed to enjoy it, folks. More than that, you're meant to. God created you on purpose—for *this* purpose.

Be Like Him in His Character

But there's more to glorifying God than being like him in his joy. Remember, God shared his glory because of who he is—generous, loving, other-centered. Being made in his image also means being like him in his character. God demonstrated his character in his work of creation, so he gives us a job to do.

> God blessed them and said to them, "Be fruitful and increase in number; fill the earth and subdue it. Rule over the fish in the sea and the birds in the sky and over every living creature that moves on the ground." (Genesis 1:28)

God commands us to establish his kingdom on earth. God worked to create the world and reigns over it. As self-portraits of him we must work to create culture and reign over creation as he reigns over us. Just as art reveals something about the artist, so too does a kingdom resemble its king. Establishing God's kingdom is about extending his humble, serving character throughout the world. *What* we choose to do in God's world isn't the be-all and end-all. He gives us freedom to eat from "any tree in the garden" that is good for us (Genesis 2:16). God gives us desires and concerns and gifts and opportunities and, most importantly, the freedom to go and pursue them for his glory.

You like working with kids? Great. Why not become a teacher? You did an economics degree? Do you fancy working in a bank? I mean, there's no pressure either way. You're free to glorify God however you want—free to build cities, draw insights, pursue relationships, develop technology, set up charities, experiment with flavour combinations, paint works of art, compete in sport, serve communities, design games, *play* games, pursue business ideas. Whatever. Feel free to go reign over creation by creating, sharing, and blessing. Just like God did.

But note this: God's kingdom is only built when we reign *in his image*. While *what* we do isn't crucial, *how* and *why* we do it certainly is. Our purpose is to be like him in the glory of his Trinitarian character. So whatever we do must be done with the same spirit of lavish generosity, humble other-centeredness, and loving service that God has enjoyed within himself forever, and that he blessed us with when he created the world. We must image his other-centeredness. That's the *how*.

And there are no prizes for guessing *why* we should do whatever we do. We do it for the same reason that God created—for his glory and the good of others. It's good that you're going to be a teacher. But teach in a way that resembles the lavish love of God for the good of your students. If you want to work in business, well and good. But you're there to work in such a way that shows that God is your supreme treasure by working to glorify him and bless others. Whatever you do, glorify him by being like him in his character.

God gives us commands on how to do this. You know the kind of thing—what to do, what not to

(Genesis 2:16–17). Without a net and some lines on the ground, a game of tennis isn't much fun. I mean, I haven't tried it, but maybe I should. Ironically, many think that these commands—God's good gift of a net and some lines for our lives—ruin the game. In actual fact, they free us to play it the way it was intended, the way it works, the way it brings us joy. These commands tell us how to be like him, to create like him, to serve like him, to work like him. Because *that's how we enjoy the purpose of our lives.* I don't know about you, but I'll take the net and lines, thank you very much.

So that's it. Most of what the Bible teaches about glorifying God can be summarized in this way: *Glorify God by being like him in his joy and his character.*

The Calling of God

You might feel let down. Like the title of this book was a good bit of false advertising. I'm with you. Picking up this book, I'd also want to know what I should go and do (not be told that *what* we do isn't all that important!) We're *do*ers, aren't we? We almost think the word *purpose* is synonymous with tasks, jobs, or callings. We pray God would reveal his will for our lives—meaning we want to know what to go and *do.* Forgive me if I have you wrong, but this was certainly my story.

I was no longer that fresh-faced first-year sipping at his cappuccino, stumbling over a response about Jesus. I now knew what I was living for. I may have become a self-exalting member of the doctrine police, but after a few years of good Bible teaching I'd at least understood that the gospel changes everything. I knew it affected every part of my life and future—of everyone's future. "What else is there to do," I reasoned, "than love and serve God for the rest of my life?" Indeed. Not many Christians would disagree. Jesus, for one, would certainly tip his hat (Matthew 22:37).

But what I meant by this was not what Jesus meant at all. In my mind this new purpose, this new calling in life, had to do with what job I would do. The phrase, "I feel called to full-time ministry," was never far from my lips. Surely this would be a purposeful life? I became fixed on the *what* and not the *how* or the *why*. I took my eyes off what God had actually said my life was for and I exchanged my God-ordained purpose for one I thought sounded about right.

I had a plan. First, I was going to move to another city to become a languages teacher. I'd earn some money so I could marry and support my wife. I'd work a few years as a teacher and then the real stuff would begin. I spoke to my new pastor about my desire to do a job like his. He was patient in listening to me, but he asked me to wait. To serve in church. To love and learn from people. But I was young. *Rest-*

less. In my discontentment, I saw my future calling as something it wasn't. Seminary became the new Disneyland. The church I would pastor would provide a platform for me to air all those ideas I had and my people would lap it up and say, "Great sermon today, pastor!" And I would say, "Praise God you found it helpful." The only thing is that I wouldn't mean it. I wasn't looking outward. All of my dreams to do God's work were about my own praise: to glorify myself and use God to that end. I called it "pursuing my calling."

You have your own story. Maybe you feel called to be a stay-at-home mom or a businessman or a coffee barista. Maybe you have no idea what you should do with your life and that's why you picked up this book… and are now about to put it down. Maybe you suffer from FOMO, the fear of missing out on what God intended for your life. Well, if you're starting to feel sleepy from all this reading, now's the time to perk up because this is important.

So long as you answer the question, "What am I for?" with a task, a job, or something you do—even if it sounds really spiritual—you will never enjoy life as God intended.

What you are *for* is about who you are *like*, not about what you *do*. You're a portrait of God. But of course, this doesn't mean God has called you to nothing.

> Nevertheless, each person should live as a believer in whatever situation the Lord has assigned to them, just as God has called them. (1 Corinthians 7:17)

God hasn't hidden your calling away somewhere and told you to go find it. He's assigned to you whatever he has put in front of you—your current situation. That's your calling, for today at least. But wrapped up in this verse is not only a reminder that our purpose isn't to do something wild, beyond our current situation; it also affirms our true purpose. Did you see it? "Live as a believer." Glorify God in whatever situation you're in. *That* is God's primary calling on your life.

If you'd hoped that by reading this book, you'd become clearer on what you should do in your five score and ten, perhaps you'll be disappointed. But I have better news for you. Whether you're a minister in Manhattan, alone in Antigua, a butcher in Bulgaria, a dad in Denmark, a widow in Warsaw, a church planter in Chile, or on holiday in Honduras, *you're not missing out on your calling.* There's no need to fret that your real purpose is somewhere else, somewhere other than where you are. No need for perplexed, guilt-riddled discontentment. God has called you to enjoy your humanity—your purpose to glorify him—exactly where you are now. Isn't that liberating?

The Full Picture

In many parts of the world, this reminder would be less necessary. Equating our purpose with our job or vocation is a very Western, first-world thing. After all, what's the go-to question when we first meet someone? "Nice to meet you, Jonny. What do you do?" Do you get that as well? Sometimes I feel like responding, "Nice to meet you too. Well, every night, what I do is dive into bed. You?"

Even if we grasp that God's purpose for our lives isn't to *do* something specific, but rather to be *like* him, we're still at risk of over-emphasizing how that plays out in whatever aspect of life we feel is most central to our purpose. But that's like doing a personality test and only answering one really important question. Even the hundred or so questions in the Myers-Briggs online tests only scratch the surface. When my wife and I last did one, we had a good laugh seeing what it claimed to be true about us. Funnier still, once each of us answered the questions and pressed "Submit," a picture appeared of a famous person with whom we apparently share many important traits. I think we were supposed to be flattered.

If there were a similar test—but a reliable one—to determine if you enjoy your life as God intended, it wouldn't ask only superficial questions about what job you do or where you live. It would be informed by

Scripture. God's word cuts to the very heart of who we are (Hebrews 4:12). It judges the extent to which every pleasure and passion, dream and desire, work and worry, response and reason, emotion and envy, task and tantrum, every creed and concern, glorify God by rightly reflecting him—being like him—in his joy and character.

A test of this kind generates a picture too. We could take one now.

» *What is your greatest love?*

» *What gets you out of bed in the morning?*

» *What makes you happy?*

» *Who are you working for?*

» *What do you dream about for the remainder of your life?*

» *What is the end point you hope to arrive at?*

» *What do you use your body for?*

» *What do you offer your eyes to?*

» *What do you do with your hands? Why?*

» *What does your schedule indicate about your life?*

» *What does the way you use your possessions say about what you treasure?*

» *To what end do you use creation?*

> » *What do your relationships say about what you value?*
>
> » *What does a simple breakdown of your bank statement show about where you're investing your life?*
>
> » *Click "Submit"…*

After I finished my last Myers-Briggs online test an image of Jim Carrey appeared…Say no more. But seriously, can we say we live truly purposeful lives *only* if our answers to these questions (and a thousand more) combine to generate a crystal-clear and gloriously brilliant image of God himself? Must we have a *perfect* joy in him, a *perfectly* outward-looking character? Maybe you feel your life rises to that level—if so, please don't waste your time with this book. It's for the rest of us dawdlers who recognize, beyond any question, that there's a great chasm between what we use our lives for and what God says they're actually for. The good news for us, however, is that no matter how faint, even seemingly non-existent, is the image of God that our lives generate, that isn't the final word. That's why there are still five chapters left.

Don't Waste It

Metaphors can be helpful, but let's talk frankly, because this stuff really matters. I don't want to be one of those guys who discovers on his deathbed that

he lived his life for all sorts of things and in all sorts
of ways that God didn't intend. I'm scared of getting
it wrong. I'm scared of missing out, of wasting my
life. I think we're all scared. So we get down to work,
plumbing the depths of our own little world. We climb
into glass boxes, doing this or that job. We're constantly on the lookout for where God may have hidden
a more fulfilling life, a truer purpose—our *proper*
calling. But here's the thing, because in one sense this
question is far simpler than we often think.

> Whether you eat or drink or whatever you do, do it
> all for the glory of God. (1 Corinthians 10:31)

This is what you need to know: Whatever you do,
whether you write to-do lists or avoid them, whether
you work or play, create or dismantle, visit family or go
shopping, drink coffee or tea, live in Sydney or Silicon
Valley, become a missionary or a miner, spend or save—
what it is doesn't matter half as much as we think it
does. God calls us to mundanity—the everyday things
of his world—and he calls us to glorify him in *how* we
navigate our lives through his world. Whether you
eat or drink, you were made to be like him in his joy
and character. He's been full, lacking nothing, for
all eternity past, before there was a whiff of oxygen
and before one drop of ink was spilled on the topic of
human purpose. And he's shared himself *with you*. So

enjoy him. Praise him. Glorify him. Be like him. This *is* a purposeful life. This, right now, *is* what you and I are for.

THREE

Meaningless, Meaningless!

It was risky ending the previous chapter like that—
enjoy God; go enjoy life! It sounds patronizing, doesn't
it? Like we haven't tried it. As if Genesis 1 has given
us a golden ticket for Wonka's land of cocoa rivers
and candy trees, so now all we have to do is run wild.
But we know the world is no chocolate factory. We've
learned that much. There are no free passes to enjoying
a purposeful life, no golden tickets.

I'm under no illusions. Since finishing that last
chapter, I carried on with life the same as before. I
came home to eat a chicken-filled baked potato before
driving to a meeting. But I forgot to praise God for the
potato, his reminder of what it feels like to be satisfied
in him. And I wasn't like him in his character when
I got annoyed at other drivers slowing my progress.
Clearly, understanding our purpose is one thing;

enjoying it in the day-to-day is something entirely different.

So I'm just going to come out and say it: it can often seem like our purpose to glorify God doesn't work. We can try our best to enjoy God and his creation, but we don't feel the joy he promises us. And the truth? No matter how much we read about purpose, even if it's from the Bible, there's still a hole in our humanity that aches to be filled. There's still a failure to relate rightly to God, to baked potatoes, and to the rest of his creation. At best we feel discontentment. At worst, despair. Our purpose to glorify God—to be like him in his joy and character—may sound amazing. But the reality of our lives makes that vision, that purpose, seem somewhere between misguided and malicious. The hole goes unfilled. It doesn't appear to work.

I don't know about you, but if God revealed nothing more than Genesis 1, I'd put my Bible on the shelf next to Charlie and the Chocolate Factory and Alice in Wonderland. But he reveals more. Far more. Scripture is real and raw about the tension we feel. Its inspired writers deal honestly with our sense of frustration, grappling to find life's purpose. For me, one particular Old Testament figure springs immediately to mind.

The Problem of Purpose

The book of Ecclesiastes introduces us to a guy called Qoholet. Weird name, I know, but it just means *teacher*. It's probably King Solomon's choice of a pseudonym. Anyway, we see in Ecclesiastes that Qoholet desperately wanted to enjoy the purpose of life. So he went looking for it. He must have read Genesis 1 because, like most of us, he made a beeline for God's gifts of creation—pleasure (2:1), a good time (2:2), home extension projects (2:4), money (2:8), sex (2:8), popularity (2:9), knowledge (2:12), a good job (2:20), and promotion (4:16). But unlike us, this guy had the cash and position to indulge every desire of his eyes and every longing of his hungry heart (2:10). For sure, old Qoholet was the talk of the town.

And how does he sum up his attempt at filling the hole in his humanity? "A chasing after the wind" (1:14). Now, I've not tried that. Maybe we can give it a go after our net-less game of tennis. But I imagine it's pretty futile. Here's what he has to say.

> "Meaningless! Meaningless!" says the Teacher.
> "Utterly meaningless! Everything is meaningless."
> …What do people get for all the toil and anxious
> striving with which they labor under the sun?
> All their days their work is grief and pain; even at
> night their minds do not rest. This too is meaning-

> less…. All go to the same place; all come from dust, and to dust all return. (Ecclesiastes 1:2, 2:22–23, 3:20)

Qoholet says that we spend our lives trying to find our purpose. But it's like catching water in a sieve. And after our futile efforts, we die. So his main argument boils down to: *"What's the point?"* It's pretty brutal.

But the Bible doesn't avoid the elephant in the room. In fact, the elephant is on every page. God's word doesn't awkwardly skirt around the hole in our humanity. It teaches both that God has given us the purpose to glorify him by being like him, and that in this world purpose can't be found. This is the problem of purpose that we all feel. But God's word is clear. There's nothing wrong with the purpose he gave us. The problem lies with us.

The Hole in Our Humanity

We can't talk about the purpose God gave us in Eden without mentioning what happened next. You know how it went. The man and woman disobey God and sin enters the world. We don't often make a link between sin and purpose. We tend to think of sin as a bit of rule-breaking—a white lie here, a character vice there. But the apostle Paul sees things differently. "They neither glorified him as God nor gave thanks to him, but their thinking became futile and their foolish hearts were darkened" (Romans 1:21).

There's nothing wrong with our intended purpose to glorify God. The problem is that, left to ourselves, we simply refuse to do so; we don't even thank or praise him for the world he's given us for our enjoyment. This is sin. It's not that we don't want a purpose; we just don't naturally want to glorify God, which *is* our purpose. Our *only* purpose. Have you ever tried telling a non-Christian they exist for the glory of God? The less we know about the God of the Bible, the less we like the idea. The thinking of all mankind has become futile and our hearts darkened.

This isn't just a character flaw. Sin is a complete rebellion and rejection of the glorious Creator God. It's a desertion of the universe's purpose to declare his glory. It's a refusal to accept our purpose, to accept the God who defines and fills our humanity. And this deserves punishment. In a way, then, God has given humanity what we foolishly ask for. He, who is our purpose, has cut us off from himself, starting right there at the beginning in Eden (see Genesis 3). We have been cut off from the God we exist to glorify. The hole in our humanity is God-shaped. It's God-sized.

So all of us, on our own, are utterly without God in the world. Yet our purpose hasn't changed. We still depend on him to enjoy our purpose. When Apple decided to stop putting a disc drive in their laptops, the design and purpose of my CDs didn't change. They still need a drive to be purposeful. Take it away and they're not much good anymore.

We, like CDs, don't function on our own. We are built to be pictures of God's glory and spectators of his glory, and this will never change. Without him, we're constantly seeking but never finding; we're alive but not truly living; we're tirelessly running but never getting anywhere. We're there, panting alongside Qoholet, chasing after the wind.

Sabotaging the Image of God: Joy

Our purpose to *find* joy is powered by a good and right desire—our need to fill this aching hole at the heart of our humanity. And we can only find it by being like him, looking to him, and enjoying him through his gifts. But our first parents turned away from him in Eden, and we each turn away from him every day. Yet our need remains. So in a futile attempt to regain the joy we lost, we do our best to feel full again.

> They exchanged the truth about God for a lie, and worshiped and served created things rather than the Creator—who is forever praised. (Romans 1:25)

God gave us the many gifts of creation to help us grasp his glory and goodness. The lie we believed is that these gifts could be god for us *instead* of him. That they could provide purpose for us. We swapped the Giver for his gifts. Sure, his gifts are astonishing. But they all point to him. Just as a million photographs can't replace a family member, the wonders of creation can never be God for us.

So we spend our lives filling the hole with his stuff. We believe the lie that changing the *what* of our lives will provide the *why*. Every now and then, we may feel that what we have in this moment really is all that we're made for. But the feeling doesn't last. Before long we don't feel full, and we know there's got to be more.

Sometimes we'll articulate a grand calling—to work overseas, to run a successful business, to plant a church. Or like Qoholet, we'll just fill our lives up with more sex, a bigger house, money, being liked, knowledge, status, acclaim, the next rung on the career ladder, a cause, the best food, more comfort. You name it, we chuck it into that hole. But it's water through a sieve. In desperation, maybe we flip the idea on its head. We embrace self-denial, coming to believe that getting rid of it all—climbing into a glass box and starving ourselves of his gifts—is the way forward. Of course, that doesn't work either.

You see, with futile minds and darkened hearts, we fail to realize something obvious. The hole in our lives is *God-sized*, and our false gods are tiny. We're trying to fill our own spiritual Grand Canyon with glasses of water. Maybe I have one glass, maybe a hundred. Either way, the parched canyon floor drinks it up immediately. We're left feeling thirsty again—thirsty for the endless, roaring waters of the glory of God.

Constantly chasing different *whats*—that ideal situation and circumstance when everything will be perfect—is a chasing after the wind. God's good gifts aren't God. When used as gods they become harsh taskmasters whom we must endlessly serve, yet who never deliver on their promises of satisfaction. Chasing the wind may be exhilarating at first, but ultimately it's exhausting and joyless. And so our purpose to be like him in his joy becomes impossible. By refusing to glorify God and use his creation to enjoy him, we're no longer like him. We're CDs looking at a super-thin MacBook, and finding ourselves without any real purpose.

Sabotaging the Image of God: Character

The lie that we could be filled by pouring more *whats* into our lives is only symptomatic of a far more subversive lie we believed in Eden. Satan didn't offer us some other god. He tempted us with the hope of *being* God (Genesis 3:5). And let's face it, who wants to be a spectator of his glory when you can be the lead role? (Says the kid who missed out on playing Joseph. Still, being a wise man wasn't bad.)

We were designed to build God's kingdom by reigning over creation as he reigns—to be other-centered; to bless others because that's what he does. But after Eden, we're now our own gods by default. Left to ourselves, we spend our lives trying to build our own kingdoms. Not many of us can say we've tried to fill the hole by pouring our lives out in service of God and the good of others. And even when we do say it, if all that activity was ultimately about placing God in our debt to secure eternal life, or to make ourselves feel better, then it's been a grand exercise in loving, serving, and worshiping ourselves. The ultimate *why* of our existence has become our own glory—the glory of a lesser god.

Unsurprisingly, our character is now a sad picture of this tiny, self-obsessed self-god.

> They are gossips, slanderers, God-haters, insolent, arrogant and boastful; they invent ways of doing evil; they disobey their parents; they have no understanding, no fidelity, no love, no mercy. (Romans 1:29–30)

It's hardly flattering, is it? We reign, not as God reigns, but how *we* choose. We rejected his commands on how to be like him, so very little of God's character remains evident in us. Our all-too-common disdain toward others is one obvious outcome of rejecting the image of a loving God. We now write our own code of ethics and get annoyed or offended when others transgress it. To be "winning at life," we put others down. We hoard the gifts and talents and resources God gave us to glorify him with, and become proud as our glory-pile grows bigger than those of our friends.

We don't serve the self-god as an end in itself. We serve it so it can bolster our claim to glory and build our kingdom ever higher. We no longer bless; we compete. Our personal kingdoms resemble their egocentric kings. "It's a dog-eat-dog world," we say. But actually it's more a god-eat-god world. As A. W. Tozer put it,

> Men have by nature no peace within their hearts, for God is crowned there no longer, but there in the moral dusk, stubborn and aggressive usurpers fight among themselves for first place on the throne.[3]

By searching for our humanity within ourselves, by ourselves, and for ourselves, we deny ourselves the proper purpose of being human. Because to be human is to be the image of the other-centered, outward-looking God. We're no longer spectators of his glory;

we believed the lie that we could be the lead role. "I became greater by far than anyone in Jerusalem before me," boasts Qoholet. "Yet when I surveyed all that my hands had done and what I had toiled to achieve, everything was meaningless, a chasing after the wind" (Ecclesiastes 2:9, 11). We ourselves are false, small gods. We live purposeless lives because we no longer resemble God. Not in his joy. Not in his character.

The Cursed Creation

You've probably heard it before, how God cursed creation. For sure, it's hard to get our head around how serious God's judgement is. But God wants to impress on us how huge it has been to lose having *him* at the heart of our humanity.

Think about it this way. First, God gave us direct, personal access to himself and expressed his pleasure — including his pleasure in that perfect God-and-man relationship — by giving us the bustling life of his unfallen creation. Then, when we rejected him — the very best of what he had given — he communicated his displeasure by cursing that same creation, us included. And this is something we experience daily.

> Cursed is the ground because of you; through painful toil you will eat food from it all the days of your life. It will produce thorns and thistles

> for you... By the sweat of your brow you will eat
> your food until you return to the ground. (Genesis
> 3:17–19)

God "subjected [the creation] to futility" (Romans
8:20, ESV). To be futile is to lack purpose. Do you
see what's going on here? We tipped the purpose of
the universe on its head by redirecting God's glory
toward ourselves. God highlights what we have done
by judging us in a way that mirrors our cosmic mutiny.
Purpose becomes futility. Joy becomes frustration.
Life becomes death. And who's immune from the pain
of death?

The arena in which we were to enjoy our purpose
has been cursed. God has thwarted our true purpose.
The drought spoils the harvest, the money runs out,
the workers are lazy, the womb remains barren, the
game gets boring, the work is hard, the photocopier
breaks, the garden grows weeds, the storm brings
destruction, relationships break down, the dream dis-
appoints, our bodies break. Our lives end.

You know this well, I'm sure. You know that to
achieve almost anything in this world requires the
"sweat of your brow." Getting to the end of this chapter
feels tough. It's as if the creation—the only clay with
which to forge a purposeful life—defies us every step
of the way. Purpose doesn't fall into our laps. It's an
elusive beast. And after all the frustrating work we put

into living purposefully, death brings us before the bar of God's eternal justice (Hebrews 9:27). This is the obvious, final sanction for turning the world on its head.

We did that to ourselves. Now it's all severely messed up, wrong, broken. *We're* broken.

Filling the Hole

You were having a good day before now, right? I'm sorry…kind of. I mean, it's important to focus on these things. Because I don't think many people ever believe that this is actually all there is.

This.

You know, what we have right now. *This*, a world both beautiful and broken. *This*, the messy mixture of joy and pain that we are constantly trying to rebalance. *This*, the frustration, the chase, the hole. As long as we are in these bodies, no matter what may happen in the future, no matter what we may become or experience, *this* fundamental reality is not going to change. There will still be pain. Thorns and thistles. The feeling of being cut off from the purpose for which we were made. In that sense, we won't have more than what we already have. I'm not sure many people, even Christians, truly believe that. Do you? I struggle to.

For many of us, our constant desire to be on the move exposes our underlying disbelief, our state of denial over *this*. So we move *up* in the world. Find a significant other. Relocate to another city. Change careers. Tick off milestones and accomplishments. We're on our way to purpose, aren't we? But where on earth can we find it? There isn't one donut, one job, one beach, one mansion, one family, one golf course, one charitable cause, one cultural experience, one political dream, one philosophical ideal—there isn't one tiny patch of this creation that God hasn't subjected to futility.

Where on earth can we go? Upwards, sidewards, across? Until we really accept who we are and the reason we were created, it's all meaningless, meaningless. Because our personal *why* remains the same. Because our self-assigned goal (our *functional* purpose), is still to live for our own glory rather than God's. We're still cursed, limited, incapable of finding real purpose apart from our Creator's purpose.

I know very well the frustration of trying to live with purpose when you reject the only real purpose any human being has ever had. The mundanity of everyday life just feels so unrelentingly humdrum when we were created for *glory*. From our place of denial, we see all these celebrities who have reached the top, and we imagine that life must look so much better up there. If that were us, surely then we could call ours a purposeful life? I wouldn't know. But others do.

Radiohead frontman Thom Yorke was someone who planned his route upward to musical fame. In an interview with *NME* magazine Yorke questioned his former passion and ambition.

> Ambitious for what? I thought when I got to where I wanted to be, everything would be different. I'd be somewhere else. I thought it'd be all white fluffy clouds. And then I got there. And I'm still here. I'm just filling the hole, that's all anyone does.

He isn't the only one. To name only a few, Boris Becker, Madonna, Chris Evert, Robin Williams—they all "made it" and expressed the same disappointment. "When you get to the top," explains author Jack Higgins, "there's nothing there." These are modern day Qoholets. They had everything their eyes and hearts desired. And they're still down here with the rest of us, filling the hole and chasing the wind.

God's Gracious Megaphone

I want you to do a thought exercise with me right now as you read this. If you're a Christian, imagine that you are not. If you're not a Christian, just be yourself. Now think about any goals and dreams you might have for your life, for earthly things like money, jobs, houses, romantic relationships, etc. Picture all your circumstances aligning perfectly, your every milestone being ticked off, one after another. Imagine an end point at which you'd finally be able to think to yourself: *I've made it. This is the place of purpose, where life actually works, where all the pieces fit together harmoniously.* Just make sure you leave God out of the picture.

No, I'm serious. Stop reading for a moment and actually do it. Picture your ideal future, without God, whatever that may be. Your every goal achieved. What does that scenario look like?

The hard truth God wants us to know and believe is that whatever circumstances or situation you just pictured, arriving there could bring you no closer to a more purposeful life than you are today. In fact, unless the purpose at the very heart of all your goals aligned with God's purpose, it would all be meaningless, meaningless; vanity, vanity.

Does that seem bleak? As I said earlier, the futility of life to which God has sentenced us reflects how evil our rebellion against him really was. So we wake up every day wanting the world—people, places, things, circumstances—to do for us the impossible.

That's the hard part of the reality we all live in every day. But it's not the only part. Because God is at work for good even in the hard part. The frustration and the futility, the ache and the anguish, are actually a gift. When none of the best things of this world give us purpose and satisfaction, God is graciously reminding us that we need him.

C. S. Lewis once said that God uses the pain and frustrations of living in a cursed creation as his megaphone to rouse us—to lift our heads out of the sand, to stop serving false gods, to stop trying to un-curse ourselves and instead to look up and see his glory. Continue pursuing what our hearts and eyes naturally desire, and we will keep traveling away from God, who is our only purpose. If that's how we live, the apostle says that we are "without hope and without God in the world" (Ephesians 2:12). Which is why it's such good news that God stepped into this world with a purpose: to set us free from *purposelessness*.

That is to say, the news gets better. The story takes a turn. I promise.

FOUR

Being the Image of God

Your suspicions are correct: I'm not usually the life and soul of the party, what with the whole "everything's meaningless" spiel. But you know what's coming now. This is the middle chapter in most Christian books about how Jesus Christ came to save the day, not least the world. We rejected the God of our purpose and deserve his judgement. But Jesus bore it himself on the cross for us. By this grace, God's justice is satisfied so he reconciles us to himself. Jesus restores us to our purpose. Job done. We all go home happy. Joyful. But do we?

I'll never forget Joe. He was like nobody I'd ever met. Unlike many of the other teenagers at camp, he was kind but also witty. Sitting in his wheelchair, his smile was contagious. His legs didn't work, but his heart did. He seemed genuinely joyful in the gospel. But on the last night of camp, while the others enjoyed a roller disco, he rolled himself outside without a smile. So I followed.

"What's up, Joe?" I asked, assuming his smile had faded beneath the pain of not being able to join in. I was wrong.

"I come here every year, and every year I resolve to live for Jesus. And when I get home I try. I really do. I know my faith has made me God's child, but I just can't do it." A tear rolled down his face. "Tonight, when we spoke about joy, I just felt numb. I felt tired from trying not to sin."

I wanted to share something of the joy of Christ— to be like our Lord, ministering to the needy. Instead, I welled up. It felt like God was using Joe, this paralyzed prophet, to pierce my own facade of Christian maturity. His words were my feelings. I'd read all the middle chapters in Christian books. I understood that Jesus died for me and for my refusal to glorify God. I believed that I'd been welcomed back to God, given back my purpose, and could now glorify him by being like him. I *believed* in the joy of the gospel. But I *felt* as little joy as Joe. The good news had just become news. Maybe I was doing it wrong? And yes, of course, I wasn't doing it anywhere near perfectly, but that wasn't the point. This was: I hadn't fully grasped that the heart of the gospel has nothing to do with what I was doing. Instead, it has everything to do with what was already done.

The Gospel Isn't about You

What God has done in Jesus Christ restores us to our purpose. In the gospel, we can glorify God, despite our fall from grace in Eden, by being like him. And in a sense, we can do this... perfectly.

Before I explain why I think it's legitimate to use that word, let's go back to what I realized after talking to Joe.

Sure, I believed in Jesus. But, although I wouldn't have said it like this, I thought the gospel was about me—my forgiveness, my reconciliation, my purpose. I'd changed the *what* of my life in so far as I was no longer pursuing false gods and was now trying to glorify the true God. This seems like a good thing on the surface. But the *why* remained the same. It was just another attempt to fill the hole for my own comfort, for my own sake. I was still the lead role in my life. Unsurprisingly, I couldn't find the joy of being like the outward-looking God because I was looking inward at myself. I was still chasing the wind.

In my mind, Jesus and I were sharing the stage. I was tragically failing to realize that it's much more about him than it is about me, and that only *in Christ* can I even begin to live for God's glory. For the image of God to be restored in us, Jesus had to first accomplish perfect resemblance and obedience on our behalf, and then give us the Spirit to empower us to resemble him.

> The Son is the image of the invisible God, the
> firstborn over all creation. (Colossians 1:15)

> For by one sacrifice he has made perfect forever
> those who are being made holy. (Hebrews 10:14)

Jesus came to be the image of God on our behalf, then
clothe us with that perfect image. That's how we can
be "perfect" *in Christ*—justification by imputed righteousness, to put it in theological terms—and that's
where we get the right motivation to live for God's
glory.

Jesus was and "is the radiance of the glory of God
and the exact imprint of his nature" (Hebrews 1:3,
ESV), *imprint* being the same word used in Genesis
1 when it says we were created "in the image of God."
Do you get what's going on here? He's living in our
place. If the gospel were about me, and if I could
become the image of God through my own effort, why
would God appear as a man on earth to live for us? He
wouldn't. It would be unnecessary. Jesus became truly
human to be the perfect substitute for fallen humanity.
He did what we couldn't do. He came to glorify God
by being perfectly like him. On our behalf. Not with
us. *For* us.

God saves his people for the same reason as he
created us—to lovingly share his glory with us. It's not
as though we *earned* God's glorious image in Eden.

We were given it. Just like we were given the creation which reveals his glory. Just like we were given the Lord Jesus Christ who *is* God's glory. Why do we assume that being like God primarily means doing something and not receiving something?

Second Corinthians 3:18 is a key verse in all of this: "We all, who with unveiled faces contemplate the Lord's glory, are being transformed into his image with ever-increasing glory, which comes from the Lord, who is the Spirit."

By sending Christ to be the image of God on our behalf and then clothe us with that image, God's speaking loud and clear. He's saying that becoming like him—enjoying our purpose again—is not primarily about what we're doing. It's not about our career plans and endless fretting. It's not about mission trips and church plants. Before we think about living as Jesus lived, he's telling us to step off the stage, to take a seat in the stalls and watch Jesus Christ fulfil our humanity. Then we'll talk church plants and careers. We were built to be spectators first and participants second. So that's what we're going to do together now for the rest of this chapter. We're simply going to watch Jesus reveal God's glory so we can become like him again. Just like we were in Eden. It really was never about us. Jesus was always the lead role.

The Purposeful Life

Firstly, Jesus revealed God's glory and glorified him in his perfect, purposeful life as a human being. "For this reason he had to be made like them, fully human in every way" (Hebrews 2:17). How could Jesus be our representative before God if he wasn't like us? Apples and oranges and all that. But sometimes we make Jesus into some superhuman—a "dish-plate messiah," as I say. You've seen the Christmas cards with baby Jesus in the manger. You know it's him because he's got a glowing dish plate around his head. As if he's glorious because he's some kind of quasi-angel baby. But that's not glorious. It's just a bit strange.

Jesus was a baby like your average ball of screaming skin. He became a human being—an actual man whose toenails needed cutting and who needed to freshen up to get rid of his bad breath. Surely this isn't the image of God's glory? But it is. Humanity in all its idiosyncratic rawness *is* God's glorious image—imperfectly but genuinely. Jesus in his humanity wasn't on a higher mystical or spiritual plane than you or I (the dish plate was a later addition). He was just like us. He "has been tempted in every way, just as we are—yet he did not sin" (Hebrews 4:15). And that's the crucial difference. Unlike us, he enjoyed his human purpose to glorify God by being like him as we were supposed to be like him: without sin.

For us, Jesus glorified God by being like him *in his joy.*

He embraced every part of the joy of being human. He had a body that was revived by food and water (Matthew 4:2, John 19:28). He loved a good party. And no, he wasn't there sipping at half a glass of red and nibbling a slice of quiche. He was called a glutton and a drunkard, while the self-righteous, sit-in-a-glass-box religious types starved themselves (Luke 7:34). He was enjoying God's gifts as a way of enjoying God himself. This means Jesus felt joy (Luke 15:5). And when God wasn't glorified, he felt anger (Matthew 21:12). Because of the cursed creation, Jesus wept (John 11:35).

For us, Jesus glorified God by being like him *in his character.*

He worked with his hands to establish God's kingdom. Not just by forgiving sins (Mark 2:5) and healing the sick (Mark 2:11), but also by taking a block of wood and making it useful and beautiful (Mark 6:3). The eternal Son of God worked as a carpenter to bless others. His whole life was the perfect image of the other-centered God. He didn't come to be served but to serve (Mark 10:45).

His was the purposeful life. He glorified God like we didn't and don't. He was like him in his joy and character. So Jesus' human life reveals God's glory, and when we stop and simply marvel at him, our humanity is being redeemed. We're closer to our original purpose to be spectators of God's glory. He did it for us. But of course, the whole issue of sin remains. Which is why the final act of God revealing his glory was still to come.

The Purposeful Death

Secondly, Jesus revealed God's glory and glorified him through his perfect, substitutionary death. The cross was where Jesus was seen to be the clearest picture of God's glory. We may want to share the stage with Jesus in how he lived, but there aren't so many takers for the whole crucifixion thing, right? It's through the horror of the cross that God communicates unambiguously that being restored to him isn't something *we* do. It's something he does for us. Something we can only receive. While we can foolishly attempt to join Jesus as lead role in our lives, the cross is something we can only look at from a distance. We can only be spectators of God's great purpose—to reveal to us our guilt and share with us the depths of his glory.

Sadly enough, however, there's still a way to talk about the cross that rids it of its power to change our lives. We can speak about it only in terms of how it relates to us and not how it relates to God. It's true—God's purpose was to crush the Son he'd loved for eternity as our substitute so we could be with him forever. He poured his anger out on Jesus so he could welcome us with a smile. He took our sin, so we'd take his perfect life. It's amazing. But the danger with stopping there is that we're a very small step from thinking God's purpose is all about us, and not about him. Or his glory. It's always been about his glory and the cross is no different.

> He did it to demonstrate his righteousness at the present time, so as to be just and the one who justifies those who have faith in Jesus. (Romans 3:26)

God's purpose at the cross was to show us his righteousness. He did it to reveal his glory. And by default, our unrighteousness and our lack of glory. Was there ever a better picture of our fall from glory than when we executed the glorious Son of God? Could there ever be a better image of God's other-centered character than Jesus hanging on a Roman cross so he could welcome back his executioners?

Of course, we see our guilt at the cross. But it's overshadowed by the joy of seeing our guilt being absorbed into the broken, human body of Jesus Christ, so that our humanity can be redeemed. Purpose included. We didn't do this. We can only watch him do it for us. "Where, then, is boasting? It is excluded" (Romans 3:27).

Do you see what the cross does when we don't

make it about us? It transforms us from boasting self-worshipers to humble, joyful worshipers of God. And this for having seen his glory revealed in Jesus Christ. When we marvel at him we glorify him. When we see our self-worship forgiven, we become like him in his joy. When we're looking to him on the cross, we're like him in his outward-looking character. The cross forgives us and restores us to our purpose to glorify him by being like him. Isn't that amazing?

> Oh, the depth of the riches of the wisdom and knowledge of God!.... For from him and through him and for him are all things. To him be the glory forever! Amen. (Romans 11:33, 36)

Being the Image of God

Amen indeed. But for all you average Joes out there—including myself—we can still miss the point. Sure, we can be amazed by God's grace. We say a loud *amen* to that. But then we have a shower. Or mow the lawn. And the joy is hard to hold onto. We ask ourselves a whole host of questions. *How can I get that feeling back of being loved by God? Shouldn't I feel more joy? How can I know that what Jesus did applies to me? Is my faith strong enough to save me?* But take a step back. Who is at the center of all the questions? If you're like me, the moment after you feel the joy of the gospel, you'll begin to look inward to validate your faith. We're desperate to catch that wind.

But God uses a little phrase for us who have even the smallest faith in Christ to assure us that we're reconciled to him and to keep us from chasing the wind. He says we've been "united with Christ" (Philippians 2:1, see also Romans 6:5,). Genuinely, if words could capture how life-transforming it is to be united with Christ—to be "in him" (2 Corinthians 5:21) or "united with him"—I would use them. But there aren't, so I'll give it a go with what I have.

Being united to Christ through our small and weak faith means that what's true of Christ is now true of us. Regardless of our lives. He took our messed up, glory-gravity-defying life so we'd get his gloriously righteous one. On your own, you're faithless, sinful, and joyless. But Jesus wasn't. Jesus had faith to move mountains, never sinned, and had the joy of being in the divine Trinity. In Christ, his faith, his human life, his joy are yours. It might not be about you, but it certainly *includes* you.

Our big question at the end of that last depressing chapter was this: how can I glorify God and become like him again? Here's the answer: by being united with Christ. Jesus Christ glorified God perfectly and was the exact picture of his glory. United with him, we *are* God's perfect image again. Let me repeat that: In Christ, *you are the perfect picture of God.* No ifs. No buts. You go mow the lawn, you'll still be in Christ. And in him, you'll still be like God. In all his perfection. Joy or no joy, sin or no sin, because Jesus was joyful, sinless, and everything else we're not. When God sees you, he sees the perfect image of his glory. He sees you clothed in Christ's perfection. Why? Because you're united with his Son. Words fail me.

Our Purpose, for Eternity

I never thought Inderpreet would help me grasp this union with Christ. She was the worst kid in school. Having moved to England as a baby, she could speak the lingo just fine but her dad couldn't speak a word. Needless to say, this made parents' evening interesting. In order to discuss Inderpreet's lack of progress, she worked as a mediator between her teachers and her father. You see where this is headed.

"I'm afraid I've got bad news, Mr. Dhali," I began. "Inderpreet isn't behaving, she's failing across all subjects and she doesn't care." I pause so Inderpreet can translate my words into Bengali for her dad. She obliges. And at this point, he starts smiling and nodding his head. A little confused, I continue. "At this rate, she'll leave school without any qualifications." She translates and her dad smiles again and gives me a thumbs up. Very odd. I had a funny feeling that her brother may give a more accurate translation. It was amazing how her dad's mood changed when little Gursharan stood in for his sister.

With Inderpreet as our mediator, my words had no bearing on her father's response. *Her* words did. If Christ is our mediator, our sin has no bearing on the Father's willingness to save us. Jesus is at the right hand of God, translating his God-glorifying, image-bearing life and death into ours (Romans 8:34). It's *him* the Father listens to.

"Your life is now hidden with Christ in God" (Colossians 3:3). Our God-dishonoring, self-worshiping lives that sabotage the image of God, are hidden. Christ's joyful, other-centered life and death is what now counts as ours. We can have confidence that we're not just *with* God. We're *in* God. Jesus unites us to himself through our shared humanity. And in him, he unites us to God because of his divinity. As his perfect image-bearers, we are now in God.

That means we're now caught up in the eternally existing, other-glorifying, lavishly loving community of God. God freely gives us his eternal kingdom where we'll glorify and enjoy him. We'll enjoy our purpose forever. I can't say how incredible this is going to be. It certainly beats our dreams to land the next promotion or retire by the sea.

Purpose Restored

Most Christians would agree that we can't enjoy our purpose apart from God. We can't enjoy life as it was intended while living for ourselves. But be honest. Are you characterized by the joy of knowing that your life is hidden and that Christ's life is yours? Or do you just have a new Christian set of me-centered *whats* in which to pursue purpose? Are you looking at what he's done or what you're doing? Which do you think about: how much you're like God, or how much Jesus was like God for you?

> God made him who had no sin to be sin for us, so that *in him* we might become the righteousness of God. (2 Corinthians 5:21)

I haven't read my Bible in a while. Sure. But God made him who knew his Bible inside out to be a Scripture-hater so that in him you delight perfectly in God's word.

My prayer life isn't what it should be. OK. But God made him who prayed perfectly to be prayerless, so that in him you depend on your Father in prayer.

I watch pornography, I'm stingy, I don't witness to others. Maybe so. But God made him who never gave a lustful glance, who gave up the riches of heaven, and who proclaimed the Kingdom of God to be a porn addict, a money hoarder, and a coward, so that in him you are now perfectly sexually pure, generous, and unashamed of the gospel.

My life doesn't glorify God; I'm not like him. You're right. But this is hidden. Because God made him who glorified him perfectly and was the exact image of his glory to be a self-worshiping saboteur of his glory, so that in him you now glorify him as the perfect image of God.

The world exists for God's glory. If it were down to us to restore ourselves to our purpose, we'd get the glory and be no closer to our purpose. In the gospel, we glorify God again because he has gloriously made us like him in Christ. Nothing in all creation—including ourselves in our own self-worshiping sin—can separate us from God's love in Jesus (Romans 8:39). We're going to glorify God and enjoy him forever in his kingdom. This is what I should have said to my Australian buddy when he asked. But *forever* feels a long way away. What about now? What does enjoying my restored purpose mean for you today and tomorrow and next year?

Well, I'm glad you asked.

FIVE

Enjoying Life as It Was Intended

Do you enjoy being a Christian?

I enjoy loads of things, but only when I'm using them for their intended purpose. I enjoy books, but not as kindling. I enjoy ice cream, but not as mosquito repellent. I enjoy home improvement, but not—as is often the case in my house—when it ruins the place. I really don't enjoy that. But that's a different story.

In a similar way, we can only begin to enjoy our own lives as God intended after we've been restored to our true human purpose: to glorify God by enjoying him forever. And to experience that joy for which we were created, we must understand the *now* of the gospel. How do I live a purposeful life *now* that glorifies God? Sure, Jesus died to take my sin and give me his righteousness. But *what now*? Yes, of course, we believe we'll enjoy being with God forever... but *what now*? So long as there's air in our lungs, the Christian "what now?" is the million-dollar question when it comes to purpose.

Given that we are now declared to be the perfect image of God in Christ, some people ask why we don't go and live however we want (Romans 6:1). "If our sin is all forgiven," they say, "who cares?" But no one who's truly looked to the Son of God dying on a cross for their sin can happily continue in it. Of course how we live now matters. Just read how the apostle Paul answers the what-now question of the Christian life.

> I have been crucified with Christ and I no longer live, but Christ lives in me. The life I now live in the body, I live by faith in the Son of God. (Galatians 2:20–21)

"I no longer live… The life I now live…" It seems contradictory. But the Bible's description of the *now* of the gospel rings true. Yes, Christ lived and died on your behalf so your life is hidden. And yes, your life therefore becomes radically transformed. It matters. God has a purpose for your life *now*. And it's this: because in Christ you *are* perfectly like God, the purpose of your life is to *become* like him. To become like him in his joy. And in his character. Sorry folks, no surprises here.

How Not to Become Like God

In this chapter, let's think about becoming like God in his joy.

For a while, I didn't enjoy being a Christian. And this was because I thought becoming like God meant adopting a Christian culture—reading the right books, singing the right songs, having the right answer to every theological question. I had no joy because fueling my desire to become like God in this way was the same self-righteousness behind my former desire to *be* God—a desire to be seen, loved, worshiped. And that's what rids us of joy.

It all looked very godly. I was serving at church. I was studying God's word. I was reading books. *Lots* of books. But strangely, as my knowledge of God's grace increased, the grace I showed others decreased, seemingly in equal measure. And why? Because the thing about self-righteousness is that it needs others to be wrong in order to be seen as right(eous). So I turned theology into a way of finding a standard of righteousness that I hoped would set me above others. Basically, in my corner of the Christian world, if you weren't an ESV-holding, Kings-Kaleidoscope-listening, Don-Carson-reading Christian, you may have been saved, but you weren't really like God at all. By which I meant you weren't really like *me*—the god of every self-righteous life.

In fact, my real claim to righteousness in the Christian life didn't primarily revolve around my theology but my zeal. I was zealously "living for the kingdom." I denied myself God's good gifts of creation and made remarks about the worldliness of Christians who went on expensive vacations or watched TV. John Wesley was my mentor when he said, "Leisure and I have parted." For me, joy meant enjoying God *exclusively*—even though God gave me his gifts as a *means* of enjoying him.

Rejecting the creation I was built to enjoy, I became ashamed of my own humanity. Spending money on myself, resting, or reading a novel became guilt-ridden reminders of my need for grace, instead of joyful opportunities to glorify God and enjoy being human. *What a waste of time when people are dying without Christ*, I'd say to myself. But my concern wasn't for Christ. Or those dying. I wanted others to be impressed by my zeal. I wanted their worship. I wanted a righteousness on top of the one Christ had given me.

Needless to say, my Christianity wasn't really cotton-candy and carousels. I never experienced the joy I declared from the rooftops. I resented others' joy. Didn't they know that it's "suffering now and glory later"? My bitterness grew. As did my sense of self-loathing for not loving others like God commands. I wasn't becoming like him in his joy. I'd become far less like him. Less joyful. *Less human*. I had simply rebranded my former me-centered life with new Christian clothes. And pretty ugly ones at that.

The Judaizers

I wasn't the only one. The apostle Paul wrote his magnum opus on the what-now question to Christians in Galatia, urging them to not do what I did. He commanded them to avoid a group of so-called Christians called the Judaizers. Now, these guys weren't as cool as they sound. Their answer to the what-now question sounded like they understood the cross. But they denied it by insisting that Christians become like God through adopting Jewish culture and religious practice on top of Christ. And this involved more than music, books, and the odd in-joke. All non-Jewish Christians were to be circumcised. Maybe a small detail for some, but Paul was fuming.

> Again I declare to every man who lets himself be circumcised that he is obligated to obey the whole law. You who are trying to be justified by the law have been alienated from Christ; you have fallen away from grace. (Galatians 5:3–4)

Tough love. You see, the moment some cultural or theological practice is required to become like God, you have a different gospel. And this is "really no gospel at all" (Galatians 1:7). Only the true gospel of grace restores us to our humanity and the joy of being like God. If Christ-less behavior change has become the measure of how well we image God, we're rejecting the gospel of grace; we're placing our hope and joy in building our own self-righteousness. And trust me, there's no joy there. But this is how the Judaizers had "fallen away from grace." Grace allows no room for a righteousness that we can muster up for ourselves. Not by animal sacrifice or by our sound theology. Not by circumcision or by our service at church.

And that's where the rubber hits the road for us. At least in England, there aren't queues of Christian men waiting outside hospitals to get the snip. Instead we are lining up to take aim at some brother or sister who knows and loves Jesus but falls foul of our own cultural practice or theological distinctives.

> *Have they even read their Bible?*
> *How can they (not) baptize children?*
> *Rap is hardly reverent.*
> *That church is so formal it denies the Holy Spirit.*
> *Do they even care for the poor?*
> *The NLT isn't a proper translation.*
> *They've dated for how long?*
> *Have you heard she's putting her kid in childcare?*

These are discussions worth having. But if it's fellow believers we're talking about, don't they have Christ who is our righteousness *alone*? Why do we require more than that? When we try to become like God by championing the ungodliness of others, we epitomise what God is not like. We're not like him in his joy. We're just grumpy and mean. We're like the Judaizers through and through.

Paul says the Judaizers, want "to alienate you from us, so that you may have zeal for them" (Galatians 4:17). We put others down in order to be lifted up. And at the root of that desire to be celebrated by others is the need to be declared righteous by them—a need that has been fully met in the gospel.

The apostle has a name for answering the what-now question by the kind of zeal that preaches grace but pursues self-righteousness. He calls it, "trying to finish by means of the flesh" (Galatians 3:3) instead of "by means of the Spirit." Finishing by the flesh makes you miserable; finishing by the Spirit makes you like God in his joy. The flesh denies you your human purpose; the Spirit hands it back. Here's how.

The Spirit of Change

If you've been a Christian a while, you'll know that God shapes us to become who we already are in Christ by his living, personal Spirit (see the end of 2 Corin-

thians 3:18). It's the Holy Spirit who makes us become
like God in his joy. And let's state the obvious: this
doesn't mean fitting us into some Christian culture or
conforming us to a behavior-modification program.
The Spirit made us Christians by joyfully opening
our eyes to our own lack of righteousness and Christ's
gracious offer of his. Why do we think that becoming
like God in his joy would begin by turning our gaze to
Christ and finish by turning back to ourselves? Again,
from Galatians 3,

> You foolish Galatians! Who has bewitched you?
> Before your very eyes Jesus Christ was clearly
> portrayed as crucified. I would like to learn just
> one thing from you: Did you receive the Spirit
> by the works of the law, or by believing what you
> heard? Are you so foolish? After beginning by
> means of the Spirit, are you now trying to finish
> by means of the flesh? (Galatians 3:1–3)

I certainly was. A fleshly, zealous fool. By contrast,
the Holy Spirit works for our joy, not by moving us
on from the cross but by constantly taking us back
there. *"Before your very eyes Jesus Christ was clearly
portrayed as crucified."* We become like God in his
joy when, with the Spirit's help, we remember that in
Christ we are already like him. There's so much joy in
the cross. There's the unshakable joy of being recon-

ciled to our God, our Purpose, the One for whom we exist. There is the unfathomable joy of possessing a righteousness that we didn't earn and can never lose.

Go ahead. Read your Westminster Shorter Catechism, give all your possessions to the poor, memorize Scripture, pad out your bookshelf, live sacrificially for the cause of the gospel, serve at your church picnic. These are good things to do. But if you're trying to add even a touch of self-righteousness to the righteousness you have in Jesus Christ, you add nothing and lose everything. You'll have begun by the Spirit and will finish by the flesh. You'll be ridding yourself of joy and of your human purpose to boot.

Enjoying God through His Gifts

I trust that you're with me here; finishing by the Spirit is the way to go. By the Spirit, we've been made children of God. By the Spirit, we've come to share in the Trinity's eternal joy. But for ten points, answer this: How did God enable us to *tangibly* share in that joy? How did he communicate just how joyful it is to be in relationship with him in a way that we can understand? Correct. *Through his gifts.*

Now, maybe it's just us Brits, but in our minds, being a Christian inevitably means minimizing our enjoyment of the whole theatre of God's creation. For us, it means being restricted to the key of G in songwriting and a lifetime of wearing checkered shirts and drinking coffee. Surely we shouldn't decorate our homes nicely or have seconds at dinner or watch light-hearted television. A theological tome must surely be a better use of time than watching a comedy. We don't want to give ourselves to idols, right?

Right. But by failing to embrace God's good gifts to us "for our enjoyment" (1 Timothy 6:17), we're rejecting the way God has shared himself with us. We're rejecting God. Self-righteous avoidance of what God has called "good" is at best stupid, and at worst sinful.

Finishing by the Spirit reminds us that we're already righteous in Christ and that we don't need a false piety. It frees us to relate to God and his creation rightly. We're free to embrace all of God's good gifts and earthly pleasures as little reminders of how good and pleasurable it is to be in relationship with him.

As Christians we certainly should be wise and discerning about what we enjoy and how much. I'm very aware, and you should be too, that there's a lot available to us in this age that we should stay far, far away from—anything that is clearly sinful according to the Bible or presents a temptation for us or others to sin (Matthew 5:29–30, 2 Timothy 2:22). Because yes, daily life is a matter of spiritual warfare against actual forces of malevolence and evil. But here I'm talking about things the Bible doesn't condemn, and therefore we have freedom before God to enjoy them (1 Corinthians 4:5–6, 1 Timothy 4:3–4).

The joy of soft socks, chicken fajitas, a mountain sunrise, the cool of summer evenings, sex with your spouse, friendship, the twists and turns of a satisfying melody, your daughter's smile, Pizza Hut, and a hot bath after a long walk—these little joys are little pictures of the joy of belonging to him. They're reminders of the love of God for you that he ultimately showed at the cross. They're reminders of the joy of being a redeemed image-bearer of our joyful God.

The Big Mac will taste good to your non-Christian friend. The comedy box set will be funny regardless of their commitment to Christ. But they'll go hungry again. They'll need to find new ways to laugh when the series is over. These joys are finite. But when the Big Mac becomes a picture of our infinite satisfaction in Christ, it tastes so much better. The Big Mac is fulfilling its purpose. The box set can now serve simply as a trailer of the laughter we'll enjoy forever—and so it's way funnier.

In this way, being a Christian isn't restrictive. It's immensely liberating. It frees us to be human again, to share God's Trinitarian joy. By gladly embracing God's good gifts of creation, we become more and more like this joyful God—the purpose for which he created us.

"It's Just Not Me"

Helen still plays heavy on my heart. We met while
working as interpreters in Berlin. We took refuge in
each other as fellow Brits. But that's about all we had
in common. She came from the "grimy North;" I was
a "soft southerner." She liked ale; I liked tea. She came
from an estate; I came from the suburbs. She "took a
baff;" I "ran a barth." She liked having fun with her
friends; my friends lived on my bookshelf. On paper
nobody would predict how well we'd get on.

Over lunch I explained to Helen the gospel of free
salvation. I warned her of God's coming judgement
and encouraged her with the joy that could be hers
in Christ. She considered it. She was genuinely taken
by this Jesus. Each day I'd ask her if she'd become a
Christian yet. "Nerrrrrrrr," she'd say, smiling. This
is South Yorkshire-ish for, "No." But the Holy Spirit
was at work in Helen. I was sure of it.

One day after work I asked her again. "So, Hells-
Bells," (an inappropriate nickname, I'll admit) "have
you become a Christian yet?" This time I didn't get her
usual response. Instead, she looked at me seriously.

"I've been thinking, riiiight,"—again, it's a north-
ern thing—"Jesus sounds amazin'. But yous Christians are all the same." She took a sip from her ale. "I
don't enjoy line dancing, or acoustic music. I can't
knit or bake. I don't want to get married when I'm 21

or have five children before 30. I'm not smart enough for all your theolology." She stopped a moment. "You see, I can't even say the word. I just don't fit. The whole Christian thing—you might call it joy but *it's just not me.*"

She was referring to the spiritual culture she'd seen at university—the one I'd become well-versed in. And this trumped what she'd heard from me about what it meant to be a Christian. Helen thought that following Jesus meant adopting some intellectual, middle-class, little-house-on-the-prairie Christian lifestyle—a kind of cultural circumcision, if you will. And in one sense, she was right. This *wasn't* her. To become a Christian sounded the same as denying her the joy of being herself. Christ would ultimately enslave her to a life she wouldn't enjoy. Or so she thought.

Freed to Be Human

Maybe you can relate to Helen. You feel the pressure to adopt the Christian culture around you which isn't really you. People talk about joy, but it doesn't feel like joy. It all feels a bit abstract. Hawaiian pizza, days by the sea, tickle fights, having an afternoon nap, English ale, Christmas time—that's the joy that's real to you.

Or maybe you're the one who avoids the things of this world. Seeing Christians enjoy so many things that you don't think have eternal value frustrates you. You do your best to "encourage" them to experience the joy of living for God alone. But you don't really feel that joy yourself. Because actually what you enjoy is to be admired by others for your zeal. Well, Paul finishes his letter to the Galatians with good news.

> It is for freedom that Christ has set us free. Stand firm, then, and do not let yourselves be burdened again by a yoke of slavery. (Galatians 5:1)

Paul is saying that abstinence from or observance of any cultural or religious practice in order to secure a righteousness of our own is slavery. But through faith in Christ you have his righteousness. And with that, you're free.

Free to enjoy your life as God intended. Free to praise and enjoy your Heavenly Father. Free to embrace the richness of his creation. Free to pursue your interests, to cultivate your understanding, to enjoy your hobbies.

You're free unto joy. You're free to be human. Free to enjoy your purpose in this world as you wait for the one to come. Free to enjoy football, Taco Bell, a holiday in the sun, daddy dates, your job, and all the things Christians can sometimes doubt they're allowed to enjoy. God doesn't only allow it; he *wants* you to enjoy being his.

Following Jesus is never "just not you." The Holy Spirit makes you more *you* than you ever were. So do you enjoy being a Christian? I hope so. If not, go eat at KFC and praise him that fried chicken is a little picture of how good he is. That's what KFC exists for. It's what you exist for.

I can hear my former zealous self pipe up, asking the right question from the wrong motive: "Is this guy really saying that the Christian life is just about kicking back and enjoying life?" Well, no. Becoming like God isn't all Butterfingers and ballet. But learning to enjoy a Butterfinger (or the ballet) to the glory of God is part of what it means to become like God in Christ. It's the joy part. But what about becoming like him in his character?

SIX

Dying to Live

Two minutes ago I walked past a billboard that said, "Your new life starts today." It was advertising shampoo. I don't know what they pack into that stuff these days, but I wouldn't bet my house on it. Or the coffee I just bought. But the huge claim of a new life and renewed purpose is exactly what the gospel promises.

Have you noticed how much of the Bible speaks about how we live? God calls us to be godly. That just means being like him in his character—living in line with our purpose. But if you're anything like every human being who's ever lived, you'll read God's commands and tend to understand them as a way to keep *him* happy with *you*. We get the purpose of godliness wrong. Or we talk about it as showing gratitude to God or it being our duty or it flowing naturally out of our joy in the gospel. There's truth in all of these. But this won't stop you from constantly fixating on just *how* grateful, dutiful or joyful you are, or ought to be. Soon enough, you'll be looking to your godliness as your hope of salvation. And if you're like me, that won't really fill you with a great deal of hope.

We often forget that *our being like God in his character is what God uses to advance his kingdom on earth.* Do you remember seeing this in Eden? God commanded the couple to reign as he reigns in order to establish his rule throughout the world. How we created, served, loved, worked, played—it was all an opportunity to be a little picture of our amazing Creator God and his kingdom. But given half a chance we went and poured it all into establishing our own little counterfeit kingdoms. Which is what we've been doing ever since. But, enter Jesus, and your new life really does start today. Shampoo or no shampoo.

And with this new life you enjoy a renewed purpose. It's still to be like God. (Don't worry, I'm not discarding the main point of the book). But by making you a citizen of his kingdom, he calls you to be his ambassador in a world that has rejected him. God has promised to use you as a little picture of himself in order to help draw people into his kingdom. Read that again. It's really important.

So here's the rub. God has given your life the highest purpose of all. He's called you, in submission to him and by the power of the Spirit, to be the very way he reaches lost souls for eternity. And he does it through your godliness, through being like him in his character.

The Picture of God

But let's ground it a bit. We're not talking about god-liness in vague, moral terms. You know the kind of thing I mean—"I avoid this and do a bit of that." Resembling God isn't vague because he's given us a crystal-clear picture of what he's like. "Before your very eyes Jesus Christ was clearly portrayed as cruci-fied" (Galatians 3:1). The clearest picture of God's character is the cross of Christ. Here his grace, justice, truth, love, humility, righteous anger, and other-cen-teredness met in one epic masterpiece of his glory. God drew people like you and me into his kingdom by an exhibition of his loving, self-sacrificial, other-centered, gracious, servant-hearted character. By his suffering. And he calls us to exhibit that same character for the same reason.

You see where I'm going here, right? God draws others into his kingdom when his people are like him in his suffering, in his sacrificial service, in his costly love. Yes, we explain the gospel to as many people as we can. But if we only explain the cross without embodying it, we're hypocrites. People don't buy that. The truth of the gospel is made visible when we're willing to lay down our lives and suffer in order to win others to Christ. Remember what Jesus said: "'A servant is not greater than his master.' If they persecuted me, they will persecute you also" (John 15:20). It'll cost us.

This is the scary truth that we Christians have to grapple with. Following Jesus doesn't mean making a few moral changes here and there. It's not a simple switch of worldview: "Whoever wants to be my disciple must deny themselves and take up their cross and follow me" (Matthew 16:24). Following Jesus means *following* Jesus. All the way to the cross.

> To this you were called, because Christ suffered for you, leaving you an example, that you should follow in his steps. (1 Peter 2:21)

Being a follower of Jesus is radical. It means giving up your claim to security, power, fame, wealth, and anything that claims our allegiance—it means giving up your life—so that others won't only *hear* of God's costly love at the cross. They will see it. And some will believe it, entering into his kingdom to see his glory firsthand.

What Shall I Do with My Life?

We all want to know the answer to that question. But God has answered it—be like him in his costly love.

So there's actually a better question to ask. *How can I display the self-sacrificial love of God to witness to the truth of Jesus right now?* Laying your life down doesn't just mean becoming a cross-cultural missionary or a full-time minister. What about the PAs? The lawyers? The single moms? The landscapers? The teenagers? What about ordinary guys and gals? Does God use us for his kingdom advance?

Yes. And I promise this is the last time I'm going to say it—being like God isn't about the *what* of your life. It isn't about what job you do. Or what circumstances you're in, or what age you are, or what you think of yourself. Being like God in his character is about *how* you do everything that you do. The question is this—in every part of your life, do you portray the message of the cross? Do you pick up a crown of gold or a crown of thorns for yourself? Do you live to lighten your load or take up the burden of a cross? This isn't just for missionaries and ministers. It's for single moms and sales managers. Nurses and nobodies. It's for you and me.

Remember, Paul says to ordinary Christians, "Whether you eat or drink or *whatever* you do, do it for the glory of God" (1 Corinthians 10:31). Whatever you do, do it in a way that portrays the glorious love of Jesus Christ at the cross. Unlike the shampoo, this really does change your life. Everything becomes a kingdom decision, an opportunity to embrace God's purpose to draw people to him. Even eating and drinking.

Are you willing to bear the cost of your reputation to speak publicly of your faith in Christ? Will you lay down your own comfort to serve the eternal needs of your church, colleagues, and community? Are you ready to see your bank statement portray the costly suffering and selfless generosity of Jesus? Will you rearrange your schedule to better reflect kingdom priorities—reading the Bible with a younger Christian, having a drink with an unbelieving friend, finding precious time to pursue your wife's heart? How does what you long for in the future, your plans and projects, your hopes and dreams, show that your ultimate hope and joy lies beyond this world? How do your conversations with unbelievers display the sacrifice of your life and an urgency for theirs? How does where you choose to live reflect God's kingdom purposes? What does resembling a crucified King mean when you get on a crowded train with only a few seats remaining? How does God taking on the cost of your sin change the way you relate to the friend who has just wronged you? Nothing in your life escapes the shadow of the cross. Ask yourself—what has being Christian cost you?

Your life paints a picture. Remember the personality test I took? Well, that was a bit of fun. But the picture your life portrays has eternal significance.

> Dear friends, I urge you, as foreigners and exiles, to abstain from sinful desires, which wage war against your soul. Live such good lives among the pagans that, though they accuse you of doing wrong, they may see your good deeds and glorify God on the day he visits us. (1 Peter 2:11–12)

The "sinful desire" to live with ourselves at the center of every decision of every day "wages war against our souls" and undermines our witness to a watching world. But when we live "such good lives" that portray God's other-centered character, he will be glorified. Not only by you in the way you live. But by the guy who sits at the desk next to yours when he turns to Christ. By your neighbor. Your tennis partner. Your dad. Your child. It could be anyone God has put around you.

Sure, many will "accuse [us] of doing wrong," as they did the Lord Jesus. But to draw some into his kingdom, he has promised to use *your* suffering, *your* costly decisions, *your* purpose to be like him. He's promised to use you for others' eternity. Could your life be any more purposeful?

Picture Perfect

Well, in one sense, yes. Because no matter how Christ-like an individual Christian is, they can never be the best picture of the triune God so long as they're on their own. John Calvin famously said there's no salvation outside of the church. In the same way, we can't be like God in his character on our own. After all, he is by nature a community—one God expressing his other-exalting, ever-loving, self-sacrificial character among the Father, Son, and Spirit. To be like him in his character is to be one person, loving and serving other members of the community of God, the church.

The apostle Paul calls the church "the body of Christ" (Ephesians 4:12). In the world, we are the visible body of the now invisible Jesus. We're like God in that we're one church comprising many people. But it's more than that. We're Christ's *body.* His body was broken, bruised, and beaten in order to bring our healing. Paul's saying that our new purpose to be the picture of the suffering God is not an individual affair. You can only properly portray the love of the triune God when we love his people. As the body of Christ, we're free to be broken in order to minister gospel healing to God's people.

Don't let the metaphor blur how practical this is. The New Testament writers use two words to explain how we give our lives away for God's people. Google tells me the phrase "one another" appears in forty-seven separate commands to Christians on how to do church relationships. (Siri says forty-eight, but we'll let them fight it out.) "Be devoted to one another," "honor one another," "encourage one another," "serve one another," "bear with one another," "submit to one another," "spur one another on," "don't slander one another," "don't grumble against one another," "offer hospitality to one another," "*love* one another." In other words, be like God, *to one another.*

But why? Again, we're tempted to think that God kind of wants us to be nice because he's nice. That sounds good. But it's way bigger than that.

> His intent was that now, through the church, the manifold wisdom of God should be made known to the rulers and authorities in the heavenly realms, according to his eternal purpose that he accomplished in Christ Jesus our Lord. (Ephesians 3:10–11)

Let me paraphrase. You know that little Sunday morning gathering of you, Dave, Julie, Miguel, a few others, and a guitar? You are God's wisdom *embodied.* You are God's "eternal purpose." You are his chosen means of preaching and portraying the gospel to the whole cosmos—from "the heavenly realms" to Jim and Naomi next door. This is why we preach and speak of the gospel faithfully. And this is why the way we sacrificially serve our brothers and sisters must match our message. When we *one-another* one another well, we portray the glory of the loving community of God.

Others will see his glory and so glorify him. In this way, your godliness is missional.

And this is what the early church did. They not only "devoted themselves to the apostles' teaching" but to "fellowship" (Acts 2:42). They gave up their claim to their finances and their possessions to ensure that no one was in need (2:45). And what happened? You get the message. "The Lord added to their number daily those who were being saved" (2:47).

The point is this: your commitment to becoming like God in his character is reflected in your commitment to sacrificially serve the church. To serve the real, needy, broken people of God. It's not about becoming a hero. It just means getting involved in ordinary people's lives, reminding them of Christ, bearing their struggles, sharing what you have. So living a purposeful human life in the local church is costly, for sure. But if it didn't hurt one bit, we wouldn't really be following Jesus at all.

You've Died and Been Raised

I think we all know that laying our lives down for one another is part of our human purpose. I mean, Christian or not, we really dig it. That's why movie writers fill script after script with heroic tales of costly love. But let's face it. We love self-sacrifice but we don't like sacrificing *our* selves. Seeing Jack hanging off a piece of the Titanic to save Rose brings a tear to my eye. But as I wipe my eyes dry, I'm sitting there fretting that my wife next to me is eating more popcorn than me. We drag our heels against what we know to be true.

So how do we find it in ourselves to live purposefully and lay down everything for others? Well, in short, we don't. There's no power in us; it's in what God has done for us in Christ. Remember what we said about being united with Christ? We said that whatever is true of Christ has become true of us. And that doesn't mean just our final salvation, but our kingdom living as well. Our union with Christ is the power and freedom to die to ourselves.

> If we have been united with him in a death like his, we will certainly also be united with him in a resurrection like his. For we know that our old self was crucified with him... that we should no longer be slaves to sin—because anyone who has died has been set free from sin. (Romans 6:5–7)

Paul is saying that for those who died with Christ, what is there now to hang on to? Why do we still chase a life that we died to? When we were slaves to sin—incapable of living for anything other than ourselves—we died. *We died.* To keep on "living for number one" is literally to flog a dead horse. OK, not literally, but you get the point. To do so denies the fact that our old, self-centered life is no more. It's dead.

Having died with Christ, we're united with him in his resurrection. We have a new life, which begins now and culminates in eternity with him. We're no longer slaves, investing our lives in our counterfeit kingdom. Having received everything in eternity, we're free to give everything away on earth. Paul's point is simple. Our power and motivation to do what would otherwise be impossible for us is simply this: to consider our death and resurrection in Christ. You've already died, so die to yourself. You've already been raised, so live a new life. With eternal life assured, what else is there to do with our earthly lives than give them away?

One More Life

It reminds me of a scene at the end of Stephen Spielberg's holocaust epic, *Schindler's List*. Oscar Schindler was a wealthy businessman who once exploited Jewish workers. But witnessing a Nazi massacre led to Schindler's radical new resolve to use his wealth to bribe Nazi officers and save the lives of more than a thousand Jews.

In the closing scene, Schindler looks around at all the people who owed their lives to him and he whispers to his close Jewish friend, Stern, "I could have got more." Stern comforts Schindler but he breaks down in his arms: "I threw away so much money. This car, why did I keep the car? That's ten people right there.

This pin? This is gold. Two more people. Maybe one. *One* more life."

Schindler wasn't unhappy to have saved the lives of so many. What grieved him was the amount of wastage that could have been invested into what really mattered—the lives of people. Maybe one, maybe ten. Of course Schindler was a hero. But his tears serve as a vivid reminder of how we'll also look back on the way we lived in light of eternity.

Look around you. Millions of *people*. Doing life. Eating, drinking, marrying, and being given in marriage. Working, resting, playing, hurting. These are souls. And most of them are living for themselves on a path to eternal judgement (Matthew 7:14). And you who've been called, not only to eternity in God's kingdom, but to be God's means of reaching some of those people, how does that affect how you live today? Will you "wage war" against the sinful desire to live with your own pleasure, comfort, security, power, and position at the center of what you do? Or will you live purposefully, being like God in his character as you "take up your cross"?

Think about your life. And like Schindler, hate the wastage. The money spent on whatever draws your love away from God, his church, and others; the time invested in building a name for yourself; the pursuit of comfort that will seem so pointless on the day we enter the eternal comfort of his kingdom. Whatever blurs you, whatever keeps you from being a clear image of the suffering servant-God, don't entertain it for a second. How you live today may become how you live the rest of your life—a life intended for a purpose, the purpose of displaying God's kingdom by glorifying him and being like him in his sacrificial character. There are real lives at stake—human beings, spiritual immortals. That's what we'll think about on the verge of eternity. People.

People are the goal of every kingdom decision we should make while we live on earth.

The Joy of Sacrifice

It's not been long since we were talking in this book about enjoying life as it was intended. Is it really possible to enjoy life *and* lay it down? Well, if Jesus is anything to go by—and I normally find he is—laying our lives down doesn't rid us of joy. In fact, they go hand in hand. Jesus endured the cross "for the joy set before him" (Hebrews 12:2). He enjoyed a glass of red; he went to the cross. And he glorified God in both.

We all naturally believe that holding tightly on to our lives will make us happy. We want to keep our money, to squirrel away what we have for ourselves, to spend our time as best serves us, to be "winning at life." But as those created to image the self-giving God, to do this is to deny our truest possible humanity. It's to forgo our purpose to be like God in his character. Jesus told us how to find lasting joy and happiness as his followers.

> For whoever wants to save their life will lose it, but whoever loses their life for me and for the gospel will save it. (Mark 8:35)

To put it bluntly, we're wrong. Living for ourselves doesn't make us happy. In fact, it makes us sad, empty, unhuman. Sure, suffering for the name of Christ or profoundly loving a brother or sister comes at a cost. But in it we experience a deep joy that rings true with how we were designed. Jesus' crash course on how to enjoy life's purpose is to lose our life. For his glory and the cause of the gospel.

C. S. Lewis, in *The Weight of Glory*, wrote, "it must be true, as an old writer says, that he who has God and everything else has no more than he who has God only." The point is that we can have everything we're looking for in God alone. But I'd go further. I think the person who has nothing but God, having left everything to follow Jesus Christ, is actually *better off* than the person who has God and everything else. Unlike most of us, that person truly understands that they need nothing other than the God they have in the gospel. No dreams. No pension. No coastal view. No job security. No change in life circumstances. They have it all. Because they chose to lose it all.

We have to ask ourselves: *Am I willing to trust God? Am I willing to trust that I'll really enjoy true human purpose when I lay my life down in service of his kingdom?* If you are willing, people will see a joy they don't see anywhere else and will want to know what all the fuss is about. And my word, eternity spent with this God is worth fussing about. For now at least, it's certainly worth one final chapter.

SEVEN

Your Best Life Soon

"Enjoying life as it was intended?" He leaned forward and put his mug on the coffee table. "It sounds a bit… *Osteen-esque.*"

My friend Ben was referring to the *New York Times* bestseller, *Your Best Life Now.* Despite selling more than eight million copies, it wasn't really the kind of book I was hoping to write.

"No point going there, mate," he said, leaning back on the couch. "It won't sell a millionth of what his book has."

So, eight copies then. If you're the one person reading this who isn't my wife, mom, dog, or handful of closest pals, thanks. It means a lot. But no matter how many millions of people want to read a seven-step book to enjoying their best life now, that book won't be the Bible. Or a fair account of what it says. Because

God's word promises something more along the lines of, *Your Best Life... Soon.*

If the world exists for God's glory, how can you *fully* enjoy life as it was intended in a world that rejects him? How can you *fully* glorify God while there are still parts of your life that don't? For sure, God has given you Christ's perfect image; his purpose is at work as you become who you are in Christ. But in God's *new* world, the one yet to come, there'll be no more "becoming." His purpose will be complete. You'll *be* who you are—a restored human being, free to fully enjoy life as God intended it.

It's hard to see that now. But when we get there, we'll realize how much in common we had with David Blaine. We'll look back and see that so much of our lives in this world was like a futile search for our deepest humanity from inside an empty glass box. The hope of glory right was right on the other side of the glass, but we could never grasp it. But God's purpose—to bring us into his kingdom—guarantees that soon we will. We *will* grasp it. We *will* experience the purpose of being human. And it'll be far better than the best this cursed creation has to offer. In fact, according to the apostle Paul, it's not even worth comparing.

The Glory to Be Revealed

We've got some weird ideas about the new creation, or "heaven" as we often call it. We've still got the whole Renaissance art thing going on. You know, plump little curly-haired Caucasian toddlers floating on clouds and hiding their private parts. But this implies God didn't create us or his world as gloriously as he could have. That maybe we would've been better pictures of his glory if we were flying harpists, or walked on clouds. But that's not right. God said the world declared the *fullness* of his glory; we were his *perfect* image. So God's not going to make new *things*. He says, "I am making *everything new!*" (Revelation 21:5).

He means the world isn't going to become some pie-in-the-sky kingdom. It's going to be like this world, but restored. We'll eat and laugh together. We'll play sport and build cities, enjoy friendships and marvel at the creation's beauty. And we'll glorify him for it. Didn't God originally give us food, laughter, sport, cities, friendships, and beauty so that we'd glorify him? So that we'd be like him in his joy? God's purpose hasn't changed. The new creation will be like this one. But better. Far, far better.

Because any joy we have in this world comes with some reminder of the creation's curse. But not in God's restored world. I, for one, am looking forward to living in a city without poverty, eating burgers without the threat of heart disease, walking along the beach without getting sunburnt, enjoying wine at parties without drunkenness, watching England play a sport without the fear of losing. OK, so maybe the last one's fanciful, but you get the point. In this world, joy comes with curse. In God's new world, it will be joy on joy on joy. Reoccurring.

In one sense, however, God won't need to communicate his eternal joy through his gifts any more. We won't need sugar to tell us how sweet intimacy with him is, or sunsets to show how beautifully good he is. We'll see him with our own eyes.

> Dear friends, now we are children of God, and what we will be has not yet been made known. But we know that when Christ appears, *we shall be like him*, for we shall see him as he is. (1 John 3:2)

We will see him. Imagine that. The joy we were created for was never to be found in the perfect marriage, a great retirement package, a healthy bank balance, the approval of others, or anything else we pursue. The joy we were looking for was God himself. And we're going to *see him*!

And when we do, "we shall be like him." We'll be restored to our purpose as a little picture of God in his glorious joy. The apostle Paul says, "I consider that our present sufferings are not worth comparing with the glory that will be revealed in us" (Romans 8:18). The joy of God's glory won't only be revealed *to* us, but *in* us. We're going to be like him because he's going to share his glory with us as he did before. So here's the take-home point: we're not going to become ghost-like beings or flying angels. We're going to be like God again, which *means* being properly and fully human, enjoying life as it was intended in the presence of his glory.

The Perfect Image of God

But it gets better. And I'll be honest. I feel totally incapable of capturing even the smallest snapshot of the eternal love we're going to experience. This love, this perfect, outward-looking, other-centered service at the heart of the Father, Son, and Spirit isn't only going to be something we'll see, but something we'll have. God's going to welcome us into that perfect triune relationship that he's enjoyed forever.

> Praise be to the God and Father of our Lord Jesus Christ, who has blessed us in the heavenly realms with every spiritual blessing in Christ. (Ephesians 1:3)

Every spiritual blessing in the heavenly realms. Paul is saying that God's going to hold back no part of his glory from us. There'll be nothing that he's enjoyed within himself for eternity past that we won't enjoy for eternity future. We're going to love God and be loved by him in ways that display and celebrate the eternal love of the Trinity.

There will be differences, of course, because we will never *be* God, never have the infinite fullness of his abilities. We will always be the created worshipers, never the worshiped Creator. (Remember in Isaiah 14:12–15 what happened when the angel called morning star—or Lucifer, if you fancy the King James—thought he could bridge that gap? It didn't work out too well. He ended up with a new name and a pretty bleak future.)

And that means we can never *experience* things exactly like God. Our experience of every spiritual blessing—love and joy and peace and communion with one another and everything else—will be full. Full beyond anything we can possibly imagine. Full to the absolute limits of our capacity to experience. Less than God's experience, to be sure, but I can tell you this— after a couple million years we won't be passing around petitions demanding that God make us a little happier.

And "we" is the key word in all this. What God started in the church, he's going to complete. There'll be a sea of people, loving and being loved by God.

> After this I looked, and there before me was a
> great multitude that no one could count, from

> every nation, tribe, people and language, standing
> before the throne and before the Lamb. They
> were wearing white robes and were holding palm
> branches in their hands. And they cried out in a
> loud voice. "Salvation belongs to our God, who
> sits on the throne, and to the Lamb." (Revelation
> 21:9–10)

We're not only going to love God but each other. In a
way that just wasn't possible so long as sin remained
within the church. We'll *one-another* each other perfectly. I so wish I could get closer to describing the
glory of this perfect community of God and his people
than I'm managing here, but this will be a world
where there is no abuse, no loneliness, no rudeness, no
selfishness, no arrogance, no murder, no stealing, no
tension, no arguments. Just self-sacrificial love, service,
kindness, peace, security.

And let's be clear—these won't be people who've
ended up where they are by some stroke of luck.
"These are they who have come out of the great
tribulation; they have washed their robes and made
them white in the blood of the Lamb" (Revelation
7:14). These are Christians who were made like God
through Christ's death. Disciples who were increas-
ingly becoming like Jesus by dying to themselves.
Believers who, like Jesus, endured "great tribulation"
before being raised up to God's throne room forever.

And that's it, folks. God's purpose will be complete. We'll glorify him forever. We'll be like him in his joy and character—the purpose of being human. That's the best life. Not now. But soon.

The Labor Pains

As a kid, *soon* was the worst thing to hear. I didn't want Christmas to come "soon." I didn't want to arrive at our destination "soon." I'm not sure I'm any different now. With the world at our fingertips, we don't wait for anything anymore. But even if we can come to grips with the fact that our best life is coming soon, we still have to ask what God's purpose is in *this* world? Does he have one?

It doesn't look like it a lot of the time. It seems a little irreverent to say that, but it's true. We sanitize the "meaninglessness" that Qoholet, Job, and King David described brutally with pithy little aphorisms like, "God works in mysterious ways." But sometimes that doesn't cut it. Where is God's purpose in the spread of various brands of terrorism and hatred? What's his purpose in the couple who love Jesus being killed in a car accident? In the greedy getting richer? In the teenager getting leukemia? In your job loss? In your loneliness? Or just in the frustration of never being able to enjoy what you have? Is this really a God with a purpose for our world?

Yes. Yes, he is such a God. And he has not kept his purpose secret.

> For the creation was subjected to frustration, not by its own choice, but by the will of the one who subjected it, in hope that the creation itself will be liberated from its bondage to decay and brought into the freedom and glory of the children of God. We know that the whole creation has been groaning as in the pains of childbirth right up to the present time. (Romans 8:20–22)

God's purpose in frustrating the world with "decay" isn't different from his eternal purpose to remake everything perfectly. He did it "in hope" that his people would be "brought into the freedom and glory" of his eternal kingdom. God's eternal purpose is at work in all our seeming meaninglessness to say clearly what words cannot: this world is far from life as it was intended—glory, joy, and purpose are coming.

The Bible makes no bones about how harsh this world can be. And it never hides the fact that God's purpose is being worked out *through* that harshness. The apostle Paul likens the world to a woman "groaning as in the pains of childbirth." This metaphor is particularly apt for me right now as my wife, Joanna, is due to give birth to our first child. Tomorrow.

"Oh man, labor's the *worst* thing in life," said one

colleague encouragingly. I'd never before made the link between childbirth and losing to the Welsh in rugby. (American friends, imagine your team losing in the Super Bowl.) But let me ask you a question. When Joanna goes into labor, should I assume the doctors are going to try make the contractions stop? Does the pain imply purposelessness? Not at all. The pain's achieving something. It's bringing on the birth of a new creation—the joy of new life.

This is what God is doing in the labor pains of this world. This is his purpose in every fiber and moment of your pain. He's reminding you that *joy* is on its way. *Glory* is on its way. Your purpose and enjoyment of life, just as he intended it, are on their way.

All Things on Purpose

In fact, God's purpose isn't only to remind us that we'll be like him one day. His purpose is to actually get going with that transformation. That's what the second half of this book's been about. It means God's eternal purpose has broken into your daily life. Eternity is being worked out right now as you become like him. The apostle continues.

> And we know that *in all things* God works for the good of those who love him, who have been called according to his purpose. For those God foreknew

> he also predestined to be conformed to the image
> of his Son. (Romans 8:28–29)

In *all things*, God is working out his purpose to remake us into his image. Some Christians have doubted that God works in every detail of life. *Surely he's got bigger fish to fry than whether my train is delayed or who I meet in the park? Isn't he focused on, you know, the downfall of Satan and redemption of the world?* But we sometimes forget that God uses ordinary means to bring about his purpose of redemption. Sure, he can work in huge ways. But he's in absolute control, to the point of using even the most insignificant detail of your life as part of the stage on which his story of redemption plays out—the story of you, and those around you, becoming more like him.

Think about it this way. We humans don't act randomly. Remember what we said earlier—we brush our teeth, not our knees, because that would serve no purpose. We don't read books or choose what to drink by pure accident. We do things *on purpose. Our* purpose. Which is to have, we hope, a better life. That motivation comes naturally to us because we were *made* for a better life in the image of a purposeful God. So why would we think that this God—the one we were made like—works any differently?

Like us, God doesn't act randomly. In every detail of your life, he's working *on purpose*—and more perfectly and consistently than we ever could—to restore you to your intended glory. Sometimes that's in your pain. Sometimes it's in the mundane. You know this, right? God uses your son's disobedience to show you how patient he is with you and to lead you toward obedience. He works through your boss' decision to have you sit in the cubicle next to Mary because, through your witness, he'll move Mary toward the day when she enters into his kingdom. In his grace he even uses your dad's adultery, so that eventually you'll better understand the perfections of God's fatherly love.

God is at work. And nothing is wasted. All things that happen are threads of his eternal purpose. The pain and the mundanity of your life are purposeful in every way. God is using everything to get you ready for eternity. And there's no doubt that, "he who began a good work in you will carry it on to completion until the day of Christ Jesus" (Philippians 1:6). Sure, we have to wait for it. But it *is* coming—and doesn't that change the way you see everything now?

Power to Live, Freedom to Lose

It did for Teri and Nick, my sister and brother-in-law. The year 2016 was the worst for them. Teri conceived their first baby not long after us. She miscarried. But then it got worse. Tests showed that her body might never be able to sustain the growth of a baby. It's the kind of thing that makes you think, *Why would God want that? What's his purpose in that?*

And then, while processing the harsh reality of their situation, Nick lost his job. Twice. I didn't even know that was possible. So naturally my wife and I visited them in their London flat. As we sat down to brunch, Nick looked low. Obviously. But something he said stayed with me.

"We knew the world was pretty messed up before this happened, but we can *feel* it now." He added some Tabasco sauce to his fried egg. Anything goes in London.

"And we knew God was good before this, but he's going to give us a transformed world where this kind of thing will never happen. Taking hold of that has shown us just how good he is."

God is so "good"—does that seem like an odd reaction to you? You'd think they might have cursed God. He could've stopped the disaster. But the labor pains of this world were serving their purpose. Seeing the new creation on the horizon freed Teri and Nick to face the crisis and affirm God's goodness. We didn't know if Teri would ever give birth to a child, but who could say she hadn't experienced the pain of labor? And that that pain had given birth to eternal joy?

For all of us who confess Christ as Lord and Savior, really seeing his new creation right there on the horizon makes all the difference now. Without that hope, we're consigned to the impossible task of finding heaven-on-earth. Kanye West summed up this burden well in the title of his album, *Get Rich or Die Tryin'*. Or if money isn't what you hope will give you your best life now, then whatever it is for you.

> Stay beautiful or die tryin'
> Get promotion or die tryin'
> Have sex or die tryin'
> Have baby or die tryin'
> Change society or die tryin'
> Be rid of depression or die tryin'

Gain control, lose weight, receive praise, have fun, be productive, write book, travel the world, win prize, find cure—*live your best life now*—or die tryin'. The irony is thick. Because pursuing that kind of life is no life at all.

However, if you're convinced your best life is still to come, you'll be free both to enjoy or to lose the good things this world offers. Better things, the very best things, are coming. You'll be free to praise God for what he's given you. And free to praise him when he holds things back—or, as in Teri and Nick's case, when he takes them away. Free to live in the dodgy part of town, to work a dead-end job, to face your family's rejection for following Jesus, to give your money away. Free to stop throwing your time and energy into that bottomless pit called the good life. Free, instead, to take up your cross and invest in the life to come.

It's no surprise that we're commanded to, "set [our] minds on things above, not on earthly things" (Colossians 3:2). Because it's so liberating to no longer live under the pressure of mustering up heaven on earth. So freeing to face the suffering of this broken world for what it is—the birth pains of eternal joy.

God's Masterpiece

Do you remember I mentioned my Grandad, the artist? When I was seven years old my parents took my sister and me to visit him and my Gran in South Africa. We went to the beach near Cape Town on a blustery day when the sea was violent. Teri and I were messing about on the sand while my Grandad got out his palette, canvas, and oil paints. My sister, budding artist that she was, went up to watch. I followed. As was normally the way.

Having drawn a few pencil lines marking the contours of the landscape, Grandad took three tubes of paint, squirted them unceremoniously onto his palette, and started mixing. Being the British Picasso I was at age seven, I pointed out his mistake. The paint on the palette looked like a colorless mush. How could it be used to paint such a beautiful scene?

He knew what he was doing. His proficiency in

bringing about his purpose with the paint began to emerge. He skillfully worked the drab mess with his brush and applied it to the canvas. I couldn't begin to see how anything good could come from such a muddle. But in a few hours the muddle had become a masterpiece. One that still hangs in my parents' home.

If you're like me, you'll want to point out where God could be doing better with the world or with your life. But he's the artist. He's the one who painted the sky blue to declare his glory. He's the one who, in Christ, made us the perfect picture of his glorious joy and character. And out of what looks like mush and muddle, he's the one expertly repainting what we sabotaged, skillfully applying the color of his eternal purpose to millions of lives across history.

It's going to be a good day when his masterpiece is revealed, when his purpose to restore us to *our* purpose is complete, when we'll be like him perfectly in his joy and character. It's hard to remember this in the everyday. I know that. I find it so hard. So if you're going to remember just one thing from our time together, it's this: in Christ, we're going to glorify God forever by being like him in his joy and in his character. So be like him now. So long as we're in this world, waiting for the next, this is what God calls a purposeful life. A life well-lived.

Endnotes

1   https://www.independent.co.uk/arts-entertainment/art/features/
    david-blaine-london-glass-box-stunt-reaction-starvation-
    above-the-below-a8523606.html

2   Jay E. Adams, *Back to the Blackboard* (Woodruff, SC: Timeless
    Texts, 1998), p 23.

3   A W. Tozer, *The Pursuit of God*, Updated Edition, (Abbotsford,
    WI: Aneko Press, 2015), p 11

Author

Jonny Ivey serves as an elder of The Gate Church in
Birmingham, UK. He's married to Joanna and they
have three children: Josiah and Halle, who are in their
care, and Edith, who is in the care of her heavenly
Father. He is the Senior Editor of *Heirs Magazine*, a
digital platform which applies the gospel to British
culture.

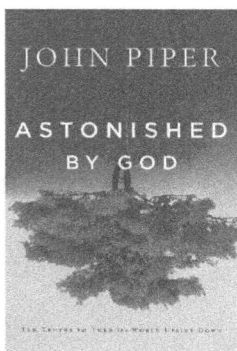

Astonished by God
Ten Truths to Turn the World Upside Down

John Piper | 192 pages

Turn your world on its head.

bit.ly/AstonishedbyGod

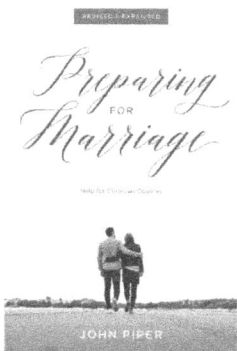

Preparing for Marriage
Help for Christian Couples

John Piper | 86 pages

As you prepare for marriage, dare to dream with God.

bit.ly/prep-for-marriage

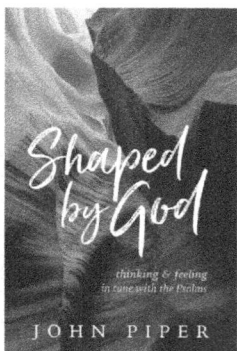

Shaped by God
Thinking and Feeling in Tune with the Psalms

John Piper | 86 pages

The Psalms are not just commanding... they are contagious.

bit.ly/ShapedbyGod

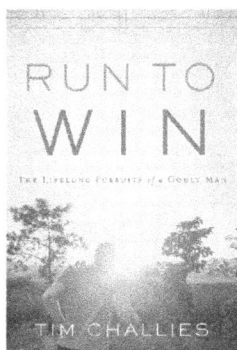

Run to Win:
The Lifelong Pursuits of a Godly Man

Tim Challies | 163 pages

Plan to run, train to run…run to win.

bit.ly/RUN2WIN

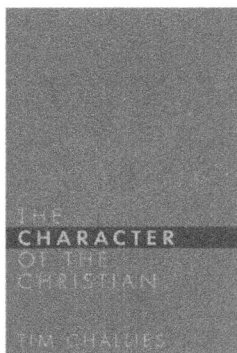

The Character of the Christian

Tim Challies | 54 pages

Learn to be a model of Christian maturity.

bit.ly/Challies-Character

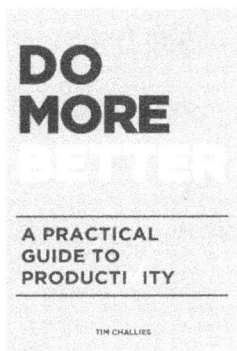

Do More Better
A Practical Guide to Productivity

Tim Challies | 114 pages

Don't try to do it all. Do more good. Better.

bit.ly/domorebetter

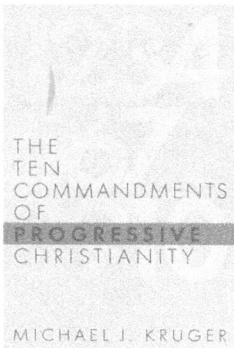

The Ten Commandments of Progressive Christianity

Michael J. Kruger | 56 pages

A cautionary look at ten dangerously appealing half-truths.

bit.ly/TENCOM

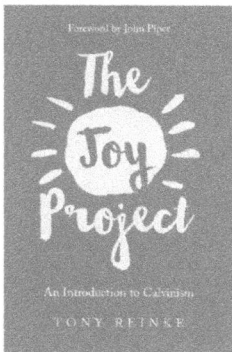

The Joy Project: *An Introduction to Calvinism*

(with Study Guide)

Tony Reinke
Foreword by John Piper | 168 pages

True happiness isn't found. It finds you.

bit.ly/JOYPROJECT

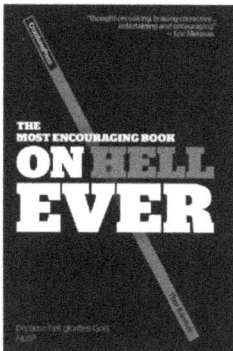

The Most Encouraging Book on Hell Ever

Thor Ramsey | 97 pages

The biblical view of hell is under attack. But if hell freezes over, we lose a God of love and holiness, the good new of Jesus Christ, and so much more.

bit.ly/HELLBOOK

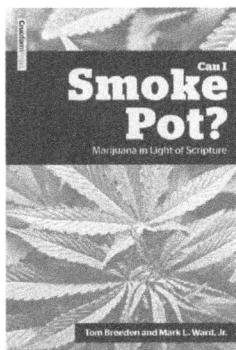

Can I Smoke Pot?
Marijuana in Light of Scripture

Tom Breeden and
Mark L. Ward, Jr. | 101 pages

*Pot is legal in more and more places.
And Christians are allowed to drink alcohol,
right? So really... what's the issue?*

bit.ly/POTBOOK

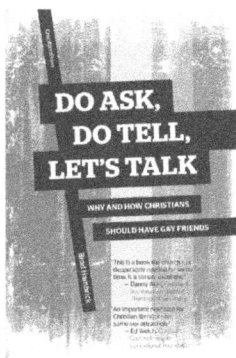

Do Ask, Do Tell, Let's Talk
Why and How Christians Should Have Gay Friends

Brad Hambrick | 118 pages

*Conversations among friends accomplish more
than debates between opponents.*

bit.ly/DoAsk

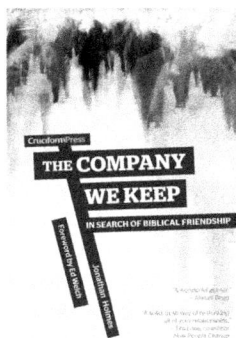

The Company We Keep
In Search of Biblical Friendship

Jonathan Holmes
Foreword by Ed Welch | 112 pages

*Biblical friendship is deep, honest, pure,
tranparent, and liberating. It is also attainable.*

bit.ly/B-Friend

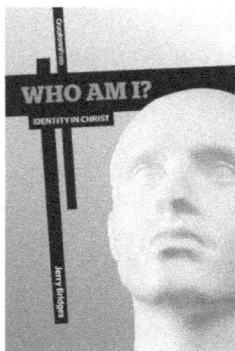

Who Am I?
Identity in Christ

Jerry Bridges | 91 pages

Jerry Bridges unpacks Scripture to give the Christian eight clear, simple, interlocking answers to one of the most essential questions of life.

bit.ly/WHOAMI

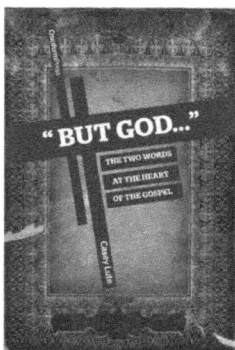

"But God..."
The Two Words at the Heart of the Gospel

Casey Lute | 100 pages

Just two words...Understand their use in Scripture, and you will never be the same.

bit.ly/ButGOD

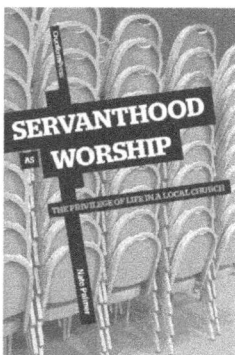

Servanthood as Worship
The Privilege of Life in a Local Church

Nate Palmer | 112 pages

Celebrating our calling to serve in the church, motivated by the grace that is ours in the gospel.

bit.ly/Srvnt

www.ingramcontent.com/pod-product-compliance
Lightning Source LLC
Chambersburg PA
CBHW061831040426
42447CB00012B/2923